TO THE ENDS OF THE EARTH

TO THE ENDS OF THE EARTH

BY JOHN PERKINS

WITH THE AMERICAN MUSEUM OF NATURAL HISTORY

FOUR EXPEDITIONS TO THE ARCTIC, THE CONGO, THE GOBI, AND SIBERIA

PANTHEON BOOKS, NEW YORK

LIBRARY OF CONGRESS CATALOGING IN PUBLICATIONS DATA

Perkins, John, 1948–
To the ends of the earth.

Includes bibliographical references.
1. Discoveries (in geography)—American.
2. Explorers—United States—Biography. I. Title.
G222. P47   910'.973   81-47209
ISBN 0-394-50900-5   AACR2

Book design by Susan Mitchell

Maps created by David Lindroth

Manufactured in the United States of America
First Edition

Of the many who helped make this book, I would like to thank especially Florence Stone, Francis Cleaves, Ruth Chapin, and the staffs of the New York Public Library and the library of the American Museum of Natural History.

John Perkins

To V.L.S.
If their roots never mingled,
Yet still may their seeds.

INTRODUCTION

Not so long ago the earth held a fraction as many of us as now, and twice as many animals. No engine roared louder than the wind, and at night the moon outshone all other lights. There were uncharted wastes, lost hills, and hidden valleys. People left their families to wander for months or years, never able to send word home. They found strange animals and fertile lands and kingdoms that had never touched their own.

Now the earth has given up its secrets. They reside within a billion human heads. And lest we forget, we keep glossy color satellite photographs of each square mile of the surface of the planet.

The change did not begin when we were hunters, stalking our quarry beyond the last place we had known before. No hunter's eyes ever saw the limits of the earth. Long after their kind had penetrated its remotest parts, the secret of the whole remained intact. But modern man, building, mapping, measuring man, has touched the ends of the earth and named the peoples and places that were hidden there.

This book documents the exposure of some of the last hidden places. It follows explorers to the Arctic, the Congo, the Gobi, and Siberia, and tells whom and what they found. It takes place mostly in the early decades of this century, when it was still possible to discover a new land or a new people, yet when the camera was available to record the discoveries with cool precision.

The explorers who went to these places risked their names and their lives for the sake of discovery. Often they died in the field. Those who survived suffered hardship and misery. A few became famous, for the public took a keen interest in the explorations of the day. And several became controversial, for, as is true of any group of people, there were villains among them as well as heroes.

It can be said that most of the modern explorers did not really discover anything, since there were people already living in the regions they set out to explore. But they were the first to draw these places into the orbit of our collective knowledge. They were the first to bring us samples of the flora and fauna of these remote places. And it was from them that we first heard of unknown bands of hunters who had lived apart from larger society for countless ages.

Much of this story is told in the explorers' own words, and their photographs show us what they first saw. When they went exploring, we were caterpillars, measuring the earth step by step. Now we are moths, flying through the air toward distant lights. Of our former stage, only pictures and words remain.

THE ARCTIC

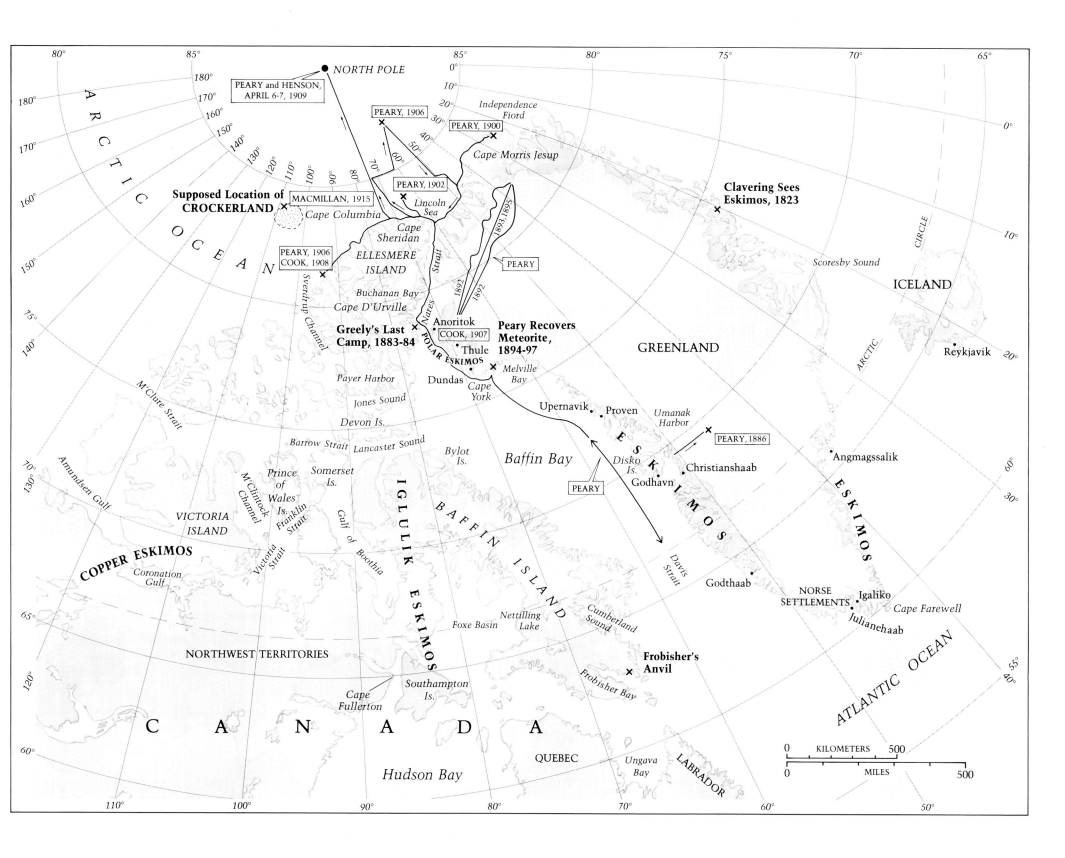

80° *85°* NORTH POLE *85°* *80°* *75°* *70°* *65°*

180° *170°* PEARY and HENSON, APRIL 6-7, 1909 *0°* *10°*

180° *170°* *160°* *150°* *140°* *130°* *120°* *110°* *100°* *90°* *80°* *70°* *60°* *50°* PEARY, 1906 *20°* *Independence Fiord* *0°*

A R C T I C   O C E A N

160° PEARY, 1902 PEARY, 1900 *30°*

Cape Morris Jesup Clavering Sees Eskimos, 1823

Supposed Location of CROCKERLAND MACMILLAN, 1915 *Cape Columbia* *Lincoln Sea* *1893,1895*

Cape Sheridan PEARY

Scoresby Sound

PEARY, 1906 COOK, 1908 ELLESMERE ISLAND *Nares Strait* *1892* *1892* PEARY

ICELAND

Sverdrup Channel *Buchanan Bay* *Cape D'Urville* **Greely's Last Camp, 1883-84** *Anoritok* COOK, 1907 **Peary Recovers Meteorite, 1894-97** GREENLAND

Payer Harbor POLAR ESKIMOS *Thule* *Melville Bay* *Reykjavik*

M'Clure Strait *Jones Sound* *Dundas* *Cape York* PEARY, 1886 *20°*

Devon Is. *Upernavik* *Proven* *Umanak Harbor* *Angmagssalik*

Barrow Strait *Lancaster Sound* *Bylot Is.* *Baffin Bay* *Disko Is.* E S K I M O S *60°*

Amundsen Gulf *Prince of Wales Is.* *Somerset Is.* PEARY *Godhavn* *Christianshaab*

70° *Franklin Strait* *M'Clintock Channel* E S K I M O S

VICTORIA ISLAND *Gulf of Boothia* B A F F I N   I S L A N D *30°*

COPPER ESKIMOS *Victoria Strait* *Davis Strait*

Coronation Gulf I G L U L I K   E S K I M O S *Godthaab* NORSE SETTLEMENTS *Igaliko* *Cape Farewell*

65° *Foxe Basin* *Nettling Lake* *Cumberland Sound* *Julianehaab*

NORTHWEST TERRITORIES **Frobisher's Anvil**

120° *Cape Fullerton* *Southampton Is.* *Frobisher Bay* A T L A N T I C   O C E A N

60° C A N A D A

QUEBEC *Ungava Bay* LABRADOR *50°*

Hudson Bay

0 KILOMETERS 500
0 MILES 500

Under the Pole is the place of greatest dignitie.

—John Davis, 1595

"If I had faculty to my will, the first thing that I would understand," declared a British adventurer to King Henry VIII, "is if our seas northward be navigable to the Pole or no." The question was not answered until April 6, 1909, when Robert E. Peary, with his black aide and four Eskimos, became the first to reach the North Pole. That one day had cost Peary nine of his toes, twenty-three years of his life, and the lives of two companions. It ended four centuries of effort by men from a dozen nations during which a score of ships and several hundred lives had been lost.

No one else since has ever reached the North Pole without mechanical support, but Peary returned to neither recognition nor reward. While he was gone someone claimed to have conquered the Pole before him. To this Peary responded that he had discovered the Pole "for the sake of the accomplishment, not for any hopes of reward or honor."

For a base, Peary chose the northwest shores of Greenland. This is the home of the Polar Eskimos, the most northerly inhabitants of the world. Until the last century, they had lived in almost perfect isolation, cut off from their southern tribesmen by the numberless crevasses of a glacier two hundred miles wide.

The photograph shows pack ice in the foreground. It forms when the sea freezes. Beyond the pack ice are icebergs, which are formed on land and pushed into the sea by advancing glaciers. In the center background the coast seems to recede; the mountainous shapes may be more icebergs or even a mirage. The sledges belong to the Polar Eskimos, who are visiting the ship on which the photographer stands. Their dog teams are tethered away from each other; otherwise, they would fight.

▸▸▸ *Greenland, northwest coast; 1911. Professor Donald B. Mac-Millan, photographer. Photograph courtesy of The American Museum of Natural History.*

We saw one of the great islands of ice overturne, which was a good warning to
us, not to come nigh them or within their reach. Some of our men this day fell sicke,
I will not say it was for feare, although I saw small signe of other griefe.

—Abacuk Prickett, Hudson's fourth voyage, 1610

Writing to Henry VIII, a Bristol merchant asserted that it was possible to pass through the polar region "without great danger, difficulty and peril; for past this little way which they named so dangerous, they come to the pole. It is clear from thenceforth the seas and lands are as temperate as in these parts."

The merchant's optimism cost him his life. He sailed north with three ships in 1527 and was never seen again.

In reality, the North Pole is in the middle of the Arctic Ocean, where the waters are covered with ice varying in thickness from several feet to over a hundred. The ice forms a great disk, over a thousand miles in diameter, that moves constantly, drawn by currents, tides, and winds. Nowhere on the planet is a larger mass of solid matter in visible motion.

The land nearest to the Pole is four hundred miles away at the northernmost shores of Greenland and adjacent Ellesmere Island. At that latitude, snow and ice are perpet-ual except in the narrow channel separating the two islands, where in good years the ice breaks into huge pieces and spills southward in the summer. It is then that a skillful navigator, with luck and a stout vessel, may sail north through the channel to the edge of the frozen Arctic Ocean. To reach the Pole from there one must cross the floating ice cap. Until the time of airplanes and submarines, the only way to do this was on foot.

►►► '*The* Panther *firing up to escape being forced onto the Berg, as the ice field was swinging towards the Berg which was grounded.' Melville Bay, northwest Greenland; 1869. Dunmore and Critcherson, photographers for William Bradford. The iceberg is much farther from the ship than it seems; Bradford noted that it was 275 feet high and a third of a mile long and was grounded in 500 feet of water. Photograph courtesy of Janet Lehr.*

He called the land, that he had found, Greenland; for he said, that might
attract men thither, when the land had a fine name.

—"The Saga of Eric the Red," referring to Leif Ericsson, ca. 1395

One thing is certain: the settlement of Greenland in the Middle Ages by the Vikings is no fable. Of that ancient colony, there still exist contemporary records, papal letters, and grants of land. Near Julianehaab on the south coast stand the Norse ruins of Ericsfiord, called by the Eskimos "Igaliko," or "fiord of deserted homes," and seven hundred miles to the north a runic stone dated A.D. 1135 was found in 1824 by an English explorer, Sir William Parry.

In the fourteenth century the Greenland colony disappeared, after lasting for nearly as long as Europeans have now been in America. One legend claims that the settlers were removed to help repopulate Norway after the Black Death in 1349. Still current among the Eskimos of southwestern Greenland is a story in which the Norse, like the Trojans, were overwhelmed by Eskimos who had approached hidden in a skin-covered raft made to look like an iceberg. Putting legend aside, we can reason that the Asiatic hunters displaced the European farmers because survival is more certain with a hunting season of nine months than with a growing season of two.

Far to the west of Greenland, near Coronation Gulf in Canada's Northwest Territories, the American anthropologist Vilhjalmur Stefansson met natives in 1910 "who took him for an Eskimo himself, because he spoke the Eskimo tongue, altogether heedless of his appearance, which of course was that of a white man. When he asked them how it was they could not see at once that he was not an Eskimo, they answered that he did not look very much different from some of the Eskimos of Victoria Land, where it was very common to find people with grey eyes and fair hair and beard."

Stefansson located the tribe, many of whom were indeed fair. The man on the right in the photograph has reddish hair and grey eyes. It is improbable that descendants of the Norse colonists could have strayed so far from Greenland. Yet none from the Coronation Gulf band had ever seen whites before; and for thousands of miles to the south, east, and west the inhabitants were universally dark-haired and dark-eyed.

▶▶▶ *'Eskimo Men.' Coronation Gulf, Northwest Territories, Canada; May 1911. Vilhjalmur Stefansson, photographer. The man on the right wears wooden snow-goggles to protect against the sun's glare. Photograph courtesy of The American Museum of Natural History.*

As the heate in all clymates is indurable, by the eternall ordinance of the creatour, so likewise is the cold sufferable by his everlasting decree, for otherwise nature should bee monstrous and vaynely created.

—John Davis, 1595

We do not know why the Eskimos live where they do, and how they developed their ice culture we can only guess. But once they had learned to hunt on the ice, burn blubber, and make igloos, a vast region was opened to them where hitherto no humans could live.

From the Siberian coast, where thousands of Eskimos remain, they spread across half the world's Arctic fringe to Greenland. They wandered so widely, wrote Knud Rasmussen, the Danish explorer, "simply because their means of existence, and the number of animals to be caught, demanded that they must fly away from each other. It took a large stretch of ground to provide the single individual with the necessaries of life; the fewer the hunters the better were the chances, so they migrated along the coasts in little flocks."

The Eskimos reached Greenland around A.D. 900 by crossing from the Canadian Arctic to the northwest coast, where the passage is shortest. Shunning the interior, all of which is a desert of ice, they spread down the west coast. After several centuries they rounded the southern tip of the island and moved up the east coast, where they still have settlements at Angmagssalik. In 1823 a British navy captain named Clavering found a band of twelve Eskimos on the east coast five hundred miles north of Angmagssalik. He and his crew spent four days with them. On the morning of the fifth day, he wrote, "we found they had all left us, leaving their tents and every thing behind." Since then, no Eskimos have been seen in the region.

In the 1930s Helge Larson, a Danish archaeologist, excavated the ruined camps near where Clavering had been. Larson found three styles of houses and implements. The first was like that at Angmagssalik to the south. The second was like that on the northwest coast, without any influence from the south. The third was a mixture of the first two.

Upon entering Greenland, most of the Eskimo bands had gone south. But some must have gone north and followed along that coast, where Rasmussen's expedition found only "a chaos of pressure ridges" and a land that, he thought, would never "yield game for wandering, not to mention wintering tribes." After being separated for centuries and circling around opposite sides of the largest island in the world, the two groups had met again. They lived together until, for some unknown reason, after Clavering's visit they vanished.

►►► *'Eskimos moving camp.' Coronation Gulf, Northwest Territories, Canada; 1911. Vilhjalmur Stefansson, photographer. Photograph courtesy of The American Museum of Natural History.*

If the moralist is inclined to speculate on the nature and distribution of
happiness in this world, [let him consider the Eskimos]: a horde so small, and
so secluded, occupying so apparently helpless a country, so barren, so wild,
and so repulsive; and yet enjoying the most perfect vigour,
the most well-fed health.

—John Ross, 1830

"From Kooilittuk I learnt a new Eskimaux luxury," related the English explorer George Lyon in 1823. "He had eaten until he was drunk, and every moment fell asleep with a flushed and burning face and his mouth open. By his side sat Arnalooa, who was attending her cooking-pot, and at short intervals awakened her spouse, in order to cram as much as was possible of a large piece of half boiled flesh into his mouth with the assistance of her fore finger, and having filled it quite full, cut off the morsel close to his lips. This he slowly chewed, and as soon as a small vacancy became perceptible, this was filled by a lump of raw blubber. During this operation the happy man moved no part of him but his jaw, not even opening his eyes."

But luxury has its price. "The causes of death among the men come largely under the terse western expression, 'with their boots on,'" Peary explained. "A kayak capsizes, and the occupant is hurled into the icy water; a hunter harpoons a walrus or bearded seal from the ice, a bight of the line catches round the arm or leg, and the big brute drags him under to his death; an iceberg capsizes as he is passing it; a rock snowslide from the steep shore cliffs crushes him; or a bear tears him mortally with a stroke of his paw: and so on. Occasionally in the past starvation has wiped out an entire village."

►►► *Eskimo women aboard schooner S.S.* Era, *Cape Fullerton, Southampton Island, Hudson Bay, Canada; 1904. Captain George Comer, photographer. The American explorer Elisha Kent Kane described the dress of a Polar Eskimo hunter he met in 1853: he wore a hooded oversuit "of mixed white and blue fox-pelts, arranged with something of fancy, and booted trousers of white bear-skin, which at the end of the foot were made to terminate with the claws of the animal." Photograph courtesy of The American Museum of Natural History.*

These savages were clothed in beastes skins, and did eat raw flesh, and spoke such speech, that no man could understand them, and in their demeanour were like to brute beastes, whom the King [Henry VII] kept a time after.

—John Cabot, speaking of three Eskimos he brought to England in 1494

The early voyagers brought back human captives with as little hesitation as we retrieve rocks from the moon today. The Danish admiral Godske Lindenau, with the Englishman James Hall as mate, made voyages to Greenland in 1605 and 1606, each time returning with captured Eskimos.

Here, wrote the seventeenth-century French historian Isaac de la Peyrère, is "the lamentable fate of the six Greenlanders that were brought to Denmark on the first voyage; that notwithstanding the kindest treatment and the best possible purveyance with stock fish and train, yet they often cast an eye northward towards their native country with sorrowful countenances and pitiable sighs, and at last took flight in their kayaks, but were forced to land upon the shores of Shonen by a hard wind, and so brought back to Copenhagen, where two of them died of grief. The two last lived ten or twelve years in Denmark and were used in the pearl-fishery at Coldingen, but being constrained to such rigorous labor, and that in winter too, one of them died at it, and the other fled once more, and was not overtaken till 60 or 70 leagues from land, upon which he also died of grief."

In 1612, Hall again sailed to Greenland. At his first anchorage, Eskimos were invited aboard. According to William Baffin, the English navigator, who was Hall's first mate, one of them approached Hall and "with his dart strooke him a deadly wound upon the right side, which the surgeon did thinke did pierce his liver. We all mused that he should strike him, and offer no harme to any of the rest; unless it were that they knew him since he was there with the Danes. And it should seeme that he that killed him was either brother, or some neere kinsman to some of them that were carried away; for he did it very resolutely, and came within foure yards of him."

►►► *'Eskimos, Igoolic Tribe.' Cape Fullerton, Southampton Island, Hudson Bay, Canada; May 1901. Captain George Comer, photographer. Photograph courtesy of The American Museum of Natural History.*

Now will I believe that there are unicorns.

—Shakespeare, *The Tempest* 3. 3. 22

On a voyage to Greenland in 1577, an English seaman told of finding "a great deade fishe, in proportion rounde like to a porpose, being about twelve foote long, and in bignesse answerable, havying a horne of two yardes long growing out of the snoute or nostrels. This horne is wreathed and strayte, like in fashion a taper made of wax, and may truely be thoughte to be the sea Unicorne. This horne is to be seene and reserved as a jewel, by the Queens majesties [Elizabeth I's] commandment in hir wardrop of robes."

The seaman had described a narwhal, a small whale native to Arctic waters. The narwhal's horn is really a single elongated tooth—a tusk. Its function is unknown. It cannot be essential to survival because only the adult males have them. Perhaps the males use them to impale their enemies, as they have been known to do to ships. A nineteenth-century Greenland whaler named William Scoresby, Jr. (who had a bed made of narwhal tusks), claimed to have seen the males "crossing them with each other as in fencing." This suggests that they might serve, like a rooster's spurs or a ram's horns, to establish rank among their fellows.

In 1636 the Danes brought from Greenland several narwhal tusks, "which at that time were unknown, and were sold in Russia for a great price as the horns of the land-unicorn," according to a contemporary historian. Around 1610 an English naturalist, Edward Topsell, described two narwhal tusks that he thought were from the unicorn. They were "shown in the treasury of St. Marks Church at Venice," and one "was of late sent unto the Emperor of the Turks for a gift by the Venetians." A century later the Danish kings had a throne made of narwhal tusks, which was "esteemed more valuable than if composed of gold."

But gold was common in old Peru; and narwhal tusks were so plentiful in Greenland that John Gatonbe, an English voyager, tells of Eskimos in 1612 bringing "unicorne horne, which they did barter with us for old iron." And in Peary's time the Polar Eskimos were still using them for harpoon shafts, tent poles, and sledge runners.

▸▸▸ *Narwhal* (Monodon monoceros), *adult male. Payer Harbor, northwest Greenland; ca. 1902. Admiral Robert E. Peary, photographer. "The Icelanders called it NARHUAL, signifying a whale which feeds on carcasses; HUAL means whale, and NAR, a dead body," wrote the historian Peyrère. Photograph © National Geographic Society. Courtesy of Commander E. P. Stafford.*

Where do you come from? Is it from the sun or the moon?

—Polar Eskimo addressing H.M.S. *Isabella*, 1818

In 1818 the English explorer Sir John Ross sailed to the head of Baffin Bay. There, on the northwest shores of Greenland, he discovered the most northerly inhabitants of the world. These were the Polar Eskimos, whose tiny band would send four men to the Pole with Peary ninety years later.

On August 10, wrote Ross, "eight sledges, driven by the natives, halted about a mile from us." He sent his interpreter, an Eskimo from southern Greenland named Sacheuse, over the ice to meet them.

"Holding up presents, Sacheuse called out to them, 'Come on!' to which they answered, 'No, no, go away.' The boldest then approached, and drawing from his boot a knife, repeated, 'Go away; I can kill you.' " Not intimidated, Sacheuse threw them a checked shirt. "They now pointed to the shirt, demanding what it was, and when told it was an article of clothing, asked of what skin it was made. Sacheuse replied, it was made of the hair of an animal which they had never seen." Then they pointed to the ships and asked "what great creatures" those were. "Sacheuse replied that 'they were houses made of wood.' This they seemed to discredit, answering, 'No, they are alive, we have seen them move their wings.' Sacheuse now inquired of them, what they themselves were; to which they replied, they were men, and lived in that direction, pointing to the north; that there was much water there; and that they had come here to fish for sea unicorns."

Sacheuse induced the leader to come "within a hundred yards of the ship, where he stopped, his evident terror preventing him from advancing another step. It was apparent that he still believed the vessel to be a living creature, as he stopped to contemplate her, looking up at the masts, and examining every part with marks of the greatest fear and astonishment; he then addressed her with the utmost solemnity, pausing between every question, and crying out in words perfectly intelligible to Sacheuse, 'Who are you? what are you? where do you come from? is it from the sun or the moon?' "

▶▶▶ *'Eskimo putting a sinew backing on bow, bow lashed to second piece of wood.' Coronation Gulf, Northwest Territories, Canada; 1911. Vilhjalmur Stefansson, photographer. Photograph courtesy of The American Museum of Natural History.*

> A great company of the savages stood looking into the boate for nayles, or any
> old iron, which they so greatly desire.
>
> —William Baffin, 1612

When the Danes colonized southern Greenland in 1721, they found the Eskimos edging their weapons with pieces of bell metal scavenged from the ruins of the Norse churches built there in the Middle Ages. The sixteenth-century English explorer Martin Frobisher abandoned an anvil on Baffin Island from which the lucky inheritors were still chipping bits of iron when an American explorer, Charles Francis Hall, met them three centuries later.

The Eskimos had metal, yet they were a Stone Age people. To them, metal was a better stone—harder, stronger, more malleable than any other. But stone and metal alike were seen as immutable. They neither knew how to work metal with fire, nor how to extract it from ores. It was something they found, imbedded in the flotsam washed ashore from distant lands or buried in the dirt beneath the ruins of a departed race.

When Sir John Ross discovered the Polar Eskimos in 1818, he was astonished to find that they too had metal. He knew their land was beyond the reach of other tribes with whom they could trade, as well as of sea currents carrying debris. Nevertheless, these Eskimos had slivers of iron which they laboriously bound to the hunting tools upon which their lives depended. They would not reveal the source of such a rare and advantageous substance, telling Ross only that it "was found in the mountain, was in several large masses, [and] that they cut it off with a hard stone, and then beat it flat."

Many Arctic explorers suspected that the iron came from a meteorite, but for seventy-five years following Ross's discovery nearly every expedition in Greenland searched for it unsuccessfully. By the 1890s enough steel had become available from the outside so that the Polar Eskimos no longer cared to protect their native source. Peary asked to see "Saviksue"—the iron mountain—and several Eskimos led him to a point three hundred yards from the shore of Melville Bay. There one of them dug through the snow, and on May 27, 1894, "the brown mass, rudely awakened from its winter's sleep, found for the first time in its cycles of existence the eyes of a white man gazing upon it."

What Peary saw was indeed a meteorite, by far the largest then known in the world. He labored for three summers to move the thirty-ton mass to the hold of a ship. From there the meteorite resumed its wandering, bound this time for New York City.

▸▸▸ *'Klipe-sock-suah and brother.' Northwest Greenland; ca. 1900. Admiral Robert E. Peary, photographer. One of the Polar Eskimo boys is cutting the flesh off a small walrus skull with a steel trade knife. Both are wearing bearskin breeches. Formerly, only those hunters who had killed a bear by hand wore bearskin, but with the advent of firearms nearly all the men began to wear it. Photograph courtesy of The American Museum of Natural History.*

The great and drierie strokes of the yce.

—Thomas Ellis, 1578

"I will speak of a little of the storme which fell, with the missehappes that we had, the night that we put into the yce," wrote Thomas Ellis, an Englishman who sailed with Frobisher in 1578.

"At the first entrie into the yce, our passage was very narrowe, and difficill: but being once gotten in, we had a faire open place without any yce, for the most part: being a league in compasse the yce being round about us, and inclosing us, as it were within the pales of a Parke. In which place (because it was almost night) we minded to take in our sailes, and lie a bull [able] all that night. But the storme so increased, and the waves began to mount aloft, which brought the yce to neere us, and comming on so fast upon us, that we were feigne to beare in and out, where we might espie an open place. Thus continued we all that dismall and lamentable night, plunged in this perplexitie, and looking everie houre for death from the great and drierie strokes of the yce.

"At the last, the Barke *Dionyse*, being but a weake shippe, and brused [bruised] afore amongst the yce, being so leake that she no longer could tarrie above the water, sank without saving any of the goodes which were within her:

which sight so abashed the whole fleete, that we thought verily we should have tasted of the same sauce. But neverthelesse, we seeing them in such danger manned our boates and saved all the men, in such wise, that not one perished (God be thanked)."

Rarely were Arctic mariners so lucky. In the 1880s, the two American expeditions preceding Peary's each lost their vessel and over two-thirds of their men. In 1848 Sir John Franklin, his two ships, and his entire company of 157 men were lost. Searching for Franklin, Sir Edward Belcher abandoned five ships in the ice, but saved his men. One of his ships, the *Resolute*, later broke from the ice and drifted, a ghost ship, until claimed by American whalers a thousand miles to the south.

▶▶▶ *'Brig* Constance *and* Hope.' *Umanak Harbor, west coast of Greenland; August 1896. Admiral Robert E. Peary, photographer. The* Hope, *on the right, is on her way south with Peary's party on board. A small boat can be seen below her flag. A man is in the rigging of the* Constance. *Photograph © National Geographic Society. Courtesy of Commander E. P. Stafford.*

I have seldom viewed anything with more admiration than this display of
courage and determination on the part of two [Eskimo] men, to resist the
approach of twelve [whites] to their encampment.

—Alexander Armstrong, 1857

In the summer of 1577, three English ships under Martin Frobisher continued to probe the coast of Baffin Island opposite Greenland for a passage to China, just as they had the summer before. A party landed at a deserted Eskimo camp and there "beheld (to their greatest marvaile) a doublet of canvas, made after the Englishe fashion, a shirt, a girdle, [and] three shoes for contrarie feete and of unequal bignesse."

Hoping that the clothes might belong to five of Frobisher's seamen who had been captured by Eskimos a year earlier 150 miles away, the landing party left a note at the camp. They then caught sight of a score of Eskimos paddling off in a large skin boat. The English ships forced the Eskimos ashore on a point of land, "whereunto our men so speedily followed, that they hadde little leysure lefte them to make any escape. But so soone as they landed, eche of them brake his oare, thinking by that meanes to prevent us in carying awaye their boates for want of oares. And desperately retorning upon our men, resisted them manfullye in their landing, so long as theyr arrows and dartes lasted; and, after gathering up those arrows which our men shot at

them, yea, and plucking our arrowes out of their bodies, encountered afresh againe, and maintained their cause, until both weapons and life utterly failed them. And when they founde they were mortally wounded, being ignorant what mercy meaneth, with deadly furie they cast themselves headlong from off the rocks into the sea, least perhaps their enemies shoulde receive glory or praye of their dead carcasses; for they supposed us to be like canibales. The point of lande upon the occasion of the slaughter there was since named Bloudie Point."

▸▸▸ *'Eskimos on beach with Oomiak.' Port Clarence, Alaska; 1891. Attributed to Miner Bruce but thought to have been photographed by Edward Curtis. The oomiak is the large skin boat of the Eskimos. It is used for a variety of purposes, including walrus and whale hunting. The one pictured here was propped on its side with a string of mink pelts tied along the gunnel. John Gatonbe, who sailed with Hall and Baffin in 1612, wrote, "Wee have seene one of them thirty-two foot in length, open in the toppe like our boates." Photograph courtesy of The American Museum of Natural History.*

The first igloo Peary built was square. He built it on the Greenland ice cap one night when a storm was brewing, and went to sleep inside, "only to be awakened by the roar of the storm and the snow driving in my face. The cutting drift had eaten off the angle of the igloo where roof and end wall met, and as I watched, it melted away as fine sand before a water jet." Thus did Peary learn why the Eskimos' igloos are round.

Once, Josephine Peary followed her husband into an Eskimo igloo. "I crawled through a hole and along a passage [for] about six feet. Numberless legs moved to one side, and I wedged myself through [an] aperture and into a circular place about five feet high, the floor of which, all of snow, was about two feet higher than that of the tunnel. A platform one and a half feet above this floor, and perhaps four feet wide in the middle and two and a half feet at the sides, ran all around the walls of the igloo [except at the entrance]. The middle of this platform for about five feet was the bed. On this bed sat Tahtara's mother, with a child on her back; another woman, his wife; and two children; and on the edge, his feet resting on a chunk of walrus, from which some hungry ones helped themselves whenever they wanted to, regardless of the fact that a number of feet had been wiped on it, and that it was not only frozen solid but perfectly raw, sat Tahtara himself, smiling and saying, 'yess, yess,' to everything that Mr. Peary said to him."

▶▶▶ *'Invilic natives.' Igloo interior, Cape Fullerton, Southampton Island, Hudson Bay, Canada; ca. 1900. Captain George Comer, photographer. The photograph has been exposed twice. On the left near the wall burns the blubber lamp. It was the Eskimos' only source of heat and light during the long night of the Arctic winter, and required constant tending. Being large and well finished, this igloo was clearly intended to serve as a permanent home for its occupants until the summer warmth made tent-dwelling possible. The nineteenth-century English explorer George F. Lyon remarked that on sunny days, an igloo's snow roof admitted light "in delicate hues of green and blue, according to the thickness of the slab through which it passed." Photograph courtesy of The American Museum of Natural History.*

We have a right to ask whether, for the sake of some fancied advantages to science,
some small fragments of information for naturalists, geographers, and the like, we are morally
justified in exposing human beings to the slow torture of a solitary death by famine or by cold.

—*New York Times*, July 24, 1873

The last American expedition to the Arctic before Peary began his work there set out in 1881. Twenty-five men under Lieutenant Adolphus W. Greely put ashore on the northeast coast of Ellesmere Island that summer. Leaving them with enough supplies for two years, their vessel sailed south, planning to return in 1883 to pick them up. Greely's men built a winter station from which they reconnoitered along the unknown northern coasts of Greenland and Ellesmere Island. Two of them sledged farther north than anyone had been before, winning the title that had been held by a string of Englishmen for the last three centuries.

But the ship that was to pick them up was crushed in the ice as it sailed north in 1883. A second vessel tried to get through, and failed. The Arctic summer waned, and Greely's party realized that no one would reach them that year. To have a better chance at being rescued, they set up a new camp several hundred miles farther south. For food, they planned to hunt wild animals; but only after it was too late to move again did they discover that they had relocated in a region scarce in game. Greely wrote in his journal, "I foresee a winter of starvation, suffering, and probably death for some."

The party fed on sea birds and brine shrimp for several months. After that, wrote one, "I ate my own boots and part of an old pair of pants." Greely recorded a typical day's meal: lichen soup, "tea, and seal-skin gloves for dinner." One large man with a ravenous appetite went mad, and

Greely had him shot for "tampering with seal thongs and other food." "So much for huge men for Arctic service," commented another of the expedition.

In April 1884, Rice, the expedition's photographer, set out with another man to find a food cache left behind by the British thirty-two years before. The weak and exhausted pair walked sixty miles to where the cache was supposed to be, but found nothing. They had just started back when Rice collapsed in his companion's arms and died, "talking of his relatives and friends and of the different meals he would eat when he should have reached home."

Finally, in August 1884, a ship rescued them. Out of the original party of twenty-five, only Greely and five others were still alive. Two of the survivors later shot themselves. Greely and another went on to become army generals.

▸▸▸ *Proven, West Greenland; July 1881. Sergeant George W. Rice, photographer for the American expedition to Lady Franklin Bay. Rice's signature is in the lower right corner. The man pictured in the center is Lieutenant James B. Lockwood, who achieved a world's record "farthest north" in May 1882. Both men starved to death in 1884. Surrounding Lockwood at the Danish trading station are Eskimos, some of part-Danish ancestry. Lockwood grasps the prow of an Eskimo kayak, which is elevated so that the dogs cannot gnaw the sealskin shell. Lying on the kayaks are sealskin floats used as drags when harpooning walruses, seals, or small whales. Photograph courtesy of The American Museum of Natural History.*

Everything in my life appeared to have led up to this day.

—Robert E. Peary, 1908

On July 7, 1908, the men wore white. It was the hottest day in New York in years, with thirteen deaths and seventy-two cases of heat prostration. Peary's expedition was poised to sail for the Pole. While his ship *Roosevelt* lay moored in Long Island Sound, he lunched with his close friend Theodore Roosevelt at the president's home in Oyster Bay. Later, the president toured the ship and shook hands with every member of the crew. As he went ashore he said, "I believe in you, Peary, and I believe in your success." Then the expedition got under way.

This was to be Peary's sixth attempt to reach the Pole. He began his Arctic explorations with a summer reconnaissance in Greenland in 1886, when he was thirty. In 1891 he spent the winter in Greenland. The following spring he crossed the inland ice near its northern extremity and proved that Greenland was an island, rather than an Arctic continent extending to the Pole. He duplicated this twelve-hundred-mile journey in 1895, but was forced to eat all but one of his thirty-five dogs to keep from starving on his return. In 1898 he began a four-and-a-quarter-year expedition aimed at reaching the Pole. Each spring for four years Peary made a try, but despite his twice breaking the record "northing," his best effort fell short by 343 miles. All but one of his toes were frozen off in January 1899. In 1906, at the age of forty-nine, he sledged to yet another record and nearly starved to death out on the polar sea when his party was cut off from the land by a large crack in the ice. In 1907 his patron, Morris K. Jesup, died, and his ship was idled for an extra year because the contractors repairing it had defaulted. "For a time it seemed as if this were the end of everything. Nor was it much help that there was no lack of well-meaning persons who were willing to assure me that the year's delay and Mr. Jesup's death were warnings indicating that I should never find the Pole.

"Yet, when I gathered myself together and faced the situation squarely, I realized that the project was something too big to die; that it never in the great scheme of things would be allowed to fall through."

►►► *'Sledges working up steep grade.' Near Anoritok, northwest Greenland; June 1915. Professor Donald B. MacMillan, photographer. Anoritok was where Frederick A. Cook made his camp in 1907 before trying for the Pole. Photograph courtesy of The American Museum of Natural History.*

> I knew it was my last game upon the great Arctic chess-board.
> It was win this time or be forever defeated.
>
> —Peary, 1910

When he went north in 1908, Peary knew all the moves by heart. In the late summer he planned to sail his ship as far as possible towards the frozen Arctic Ocean. On the way, he would pick up fifty or sixty Polar Eskimos to help him with the work to follow. Throughout the fall, he would hunt walrus, musk ox, bear, and caribou to ensure that the expedition had fresh meat for the coming winter. He would buy dogs from the Eskimos, enough to allow for 60 percent losses. Then, near the northernmost point of land, he intended to set up a well-supplied base camp from which he would stage his eight-hundred-mile dash over the ice to the Pole and back.

This dash was the crucial move. Peary judged that it could succeed only if accomplished in less than a hundred days in the early spring, when the sun was high enough to shed some light but not warm enough to crack the ice and expose channels of open water—called leads—that his sledges could not cross.

During the dash, Peary and his men would support themselves with supplies hauled on their sledges. They would each eat a pound of pemmican, a pound of biscuit, and a few ounces of condensed milk and tea per day; nothing more. The dogs would get a pound of pemmican. Even on these concentrated rations, a driver and his dog team could not carry enough food on one sledge to get them to the Pole and back again. Extra supplies could not be stored along the route because of the constant shifting of the ice. Instead, Peary would have to rely on support teams who would start out with the main party and then turn back, leaving their spare rations with those who went on.

By February 28, 1909, the preliminary moves had been made. Peary had twenty-four men, eighteen of whom were Eskimos, nineteen sledges, and 133 dogs poised for a dash to the Pole.

▶▶▶ *Polar Eskimos sledging Peary's supplies ashore, Cape D'Urville, Ellesmere Island; September 1898. Admiral Robert E. Peary, photographer. The dog teams dragged 700- to 1,000-pound loads on this short trip. Photograph © National Geographic Society. Courtesy of Commander E. P. Stafford.*

Traveling on the polar ice, one takes all kinds of chances. Often a man has the choice
between the possibility of drowning by going on or starving to death by
standing still, and challenges fate with the briefer and less painful chance.

—Peary, 1910

On March 1, 1909, the dash began. Three days later, after going only forty-five miles, Peary and his men were stopped by a lead. It was too wide to cross and too long to go around: there was nothing to do but wait and hope that the ice would close together or freeze over the gap. For six days they waited. Only "one who had been in a similar situation could understand the gnawing torment of those days of forced inaction," wrote Peary.

Once before, on his way home from an unsuccessful attempt at the Pole in 1906, Peary had been forced to wait at a lead. His party of nine were starving. "Each day," he recalled, "the number of my dogs dwindled and sledges were broken up to cook those animals that we ate ourselves." When waiting became unendurable he led his men the two miles across the lead on new-formed ice. "We had already tested the ice and knew it could not support us for an instant without snowshoes. Once started we could not stop. It was a matter of constantly and smoothly gliding one snowshoe past the other with the utmost care and evenness of pressure. From every man as he slid snowshoe forward, undulations went out in every direction through the thin film incrusting the black water. When near the middle of the lead my toe broke through twice in succession, I thought to myself 'this is the finish,' and when a little later there was a cry from someone in the line, the words sprang from me of themselves, 'God help him, which one is it?' but I dared not take my eyes from the steady, even gliding of my snowshoes, and the fascination of the glassy swells at the toes of them. Frankly, I do not care for more similar experiences."

But in 1909, on the seventh day of waiting, when an Eskimo scout found a point where new ice spanned the lead, Peary once again led his men across. As they followed, Peary wrote, "I watched from the other side with my heart in my mouth—watched the ice bending under the weight of the sledge and the men. As one of the sledges neared the north side, a runner cut clear through the ice, and I expected every moment that the whole thing, dogs and all, would go down to the bottom. But it did not."

▶▶▶ *'Sledge crossing crevasse.' Benedict Glacier, Ellesmere Island; July 16, 1900. Admiral Robert E. Peary, photographer. Photograph © National Geographic Society. Courtesy of Commander E. P. Stafford.*

It is generally believed that white men have quite the same minds as small
children. They are easily angered, and when they cannot get their will they
are moody and, like children, have the strangest ideas and fancies.

—Polar Eskimo, ca. 1930

Seated on the ice is twenty-year-old Ooqueah, the youngest of the four Eskimos who went with Peary to the Pole. For his services, he was rewarded with a whaleboat, a shotgun, a rifle, ammunition, knives—"wealth, beyond the wildest dreams of Eskimos," as Peary put it. His riches enabled him to marry the daughter of the man who had been Peary's first employee among the Polar Eskimos.

On the right is "Captain Bob" Bartlett. He came from a family of distinguished seafarers who had settled in Brigus, Newfoundland, a century and a half earlier. Every ship pictured in these photographs, except the *Constance,* was commanded by a Bartlett. In 1873 John Bartlett was captain of the ship that rescued the survivors of Charles Francis Hall's expedition from an ice floe where they had been marooned for six months. Bob's uncle, Moses Bartlett, brought Dr. Frederick A. Cook's rival exploring party to Greenland in 1907. Another uncle, Sam Bartlett, was commander of Peary's *Roosevelt* in 1909 while Peary and the others were on the dash. On Peary's successful expedition to the Pole, "Captain Bob," then thirty-four years old, broke the sledge trail over the ice for three-quarters of the way, then gave the lead to Peary and returned to land. He might have gone on, but only he and Peary were capable of guiding the ship back through the ice, and they could not risk being lost together on the dash. Bartlett made over thirty Arctic voyages during his life.

On the left is Matthew Alexander Henson. Forty-two years old at the time of this photograph, Henson had been on all Peary's expeditions except the first. He was fluent in the tongue of the Polar Eskimos, and had adopted one of their orphaned children. After he came back from the Pole, Henson, who was black, could not find work for four years until President Taft gave him a clerical post in the New York Customs House. He died in Harlem in 1955.

Next to Bartlett on the sledge is eighteen-year-old Innkitsoq, known as Harrigan because he learned to sing the ditty "Harrigan, that's me." In 1909, Innkitsoq hauled supplies towards the Pole for Peary's assault team and then started back for land with another Eskimo and one of Peary's men, Professor Ross Marvin, whose heel was frostbitten. Marvin never arrived. The two Eskimos said that he had drowned when his sledge broke through the ice. But when they were baptized in 1925, the pair confessed to shooting Marvin because he had gone mad. Innkitsoq added, "[In 1909] we were all heathens, and we had among us old conjurers to whom nothing was hidden. One of them said to me: 'You have killed the white man. I know it quite well. You cannot hide it from me.' To this I only answered: 'Yes, we killed him!'"

▸▸▸ *Members of the Peary expedition on the ice of the Arctic Ocean north of Cape Columbia, Ellesmere Island, Canada; March 1909. Robert E. Peary, photographer. Photograph © National Geographic Society. Courtesy of Commander E. P. Stafford.*

There yet lurks an elusive something in the innermost idea of this hue, which strikes more of panic to the soul than that redness which affrights in blood.

—Herman Melville, on the whiteness of the whale

The heights of the northernmost land in the world had dropped below the southern horizon weeks before. Peary had been out on the ice for thirty-three days when the last support party left him on April 2. Now he and five companions were alone on the polar ice cap. "We were deep in that gaunt frozen borderland which lies between God's countries and interstellar space," he wrote. "Many a time not only was there no object to be seen, but in the entire sphere of vision there was no difference in the intensity of light. My feet and snowshoes were sharp and clear as silhouettes and I was sensible of contact with the snow at every step. Yet as far as my eyes gave me evidence to the contrary, I was walking upon nothing."

"It was so cold on this last journey," said Peary, "that the brandy was frozen solid, the petroleum was white and viscid," and the wood of the sledges was brittle.

In the morning on April 6, 1909, Peary, Henson, and the Eskimos Ootah, Eginwah, Sleegoo, and Ooqueah arrived at the North Pole. "When I knew for a certainty that we had reached the goal, there was nothing in the world I wanted but sleep," wrote Peary. "But after a few hours of it, there succeeded a condition of mental exaltation which made further rest impossible."

At the Pole they found . . . nothing. The slab of ice upon which they stood was no different from any other in the Arctic Ocean, except that according to Peary's calculations, it happened to lie that day directly over the northern axis of the world. They spent thirty hours at the Pole. Peary and Henson took a few blurred photographs of the Eskimos holding an American flag. They fed a sounding line through a hole in the ice, but it parted at 1,500 fathoms without finding bottom. Peary shot an elaborate set of sextant readings, which blinded him for days afterwards. Then they packed up and started for land, knowing that every extra minute on the ice lessened their chances of getting back alive.

So good were the conditions on their return march that they made land in seventeen days. "The devil is asleep or having trouble with his wife, or we should never have come back so easily," Ootah explained.

▶▶ *'Pressure ridge.' On the ice of the Arctic Ocean; March 1916. Professor Donald B. MacMillan, photographer. "The surface of the polar sea," said Peary, "may be one of almost unimaginable unevenness and roughness. As a result of the constant movement of the ice, great fields are detached, impinging against one another, splitting in two from the violence of contact, crushing up the thinner ice between them, and having their edges shattered and piled up into pressure ridges." Photograph courtesy of The American Museum of Natural History.*

I bring the same proofs as every other explorer, I bring my story.

—Frederick A. Cook, 1909

When the news of the discovery of the North Pole was announced, the world went wild—but not for Peary. Instead, they cheered a man named Cook. Dr. Frederick A. Cook had served in the Arctic with Peary in 1892. In 1898 he had been to Antarctica with a Belgian expedition. In 1906 he claimed to have scaled Mount McKinley, which no one had done before. In 1907 he was in Greenland on a hunting trip. When nothing had been heard from him for over a year, he was presumed lost. But then Cook reappeared, declaring that he and two Eskimos had reached the Pole in 1908, a year ahead of Peary. He made his announcement on September 1, 1909. Four days later Peary reached a telegraph station and sent out his claim.

From the Arctic, Cook's first stop was Denmark, where he stepped from his ship arm-in-arm with the crown prince. As he sat at a royal banquet, wreathed in pink roses, he received the news of Peary's claim. "We are rivals, of course," he responded, "but the Pole is big enough for two." He could afford to be generous: he was the one who got the hero's welcome. Back in America, people were trampled trying to see him. Crowds paid record sums to hear him speak. He was paraded through New York City in a two-hundred-car motorcade, while Peary's *Roosevelt* steamed into the Hudson unnoticed.

Peary knew Cook was lying. He had talked with Cook's Eskimo companions on his way south in 1909, and they had stated openly that they and Cook had traveled only "two sleeps" over the ice before returning to land. But Peary knew it would be hard to refute Cook. On the Arctic Ocean an explorer's claim was as good as his word; there was never any physical evidence because there was nothing out there but shifting ice.

In the end, it was Cook's own story that finished him. He said he had navigation records from his trip. In December 1909, the Royal Geographical Society of Denmark examined them and found them "entirely inadequate." Cook had submitted incomplete calculations. It appeared he could not navigate with a sextant, much less locate the North Pole. By January 1910, he was rumored to be traveling abroad, incognito.

Peary died in 1920 when he was sixty-four. He had lived long enough to win official recognition as discoverer of the North Pole; but the public had grown wary after Cook, and never treated him like a hero.

▸▸▸ *Northwest Greenland; ca. 1896. Admiral Robert E. Peary, photographer. Photograph © National Geographic Society. Courtesy of Commander E. P. Stafford.*

[A legend of the Eskimos] described a distant owasis inhabited by their own
race. So perfect was this spot in its abundance of game and sunlight, that he
who settled there, whether from fortune or design, never returned.

—Lieutenant Fitzhugh Green, 1918

"With glasses," Peary observed in 1906, "I could make out, apparently in the northwest above the ice horizon, the snow-clad summits of a distant land." Whatever Peary had seen out in the Polar Basin lay far to the west of his route to the Pole. He paused only long enough to note its location and to name it "Crockerland" in honor of a patron.

On his sledge journey in 1908, Cook claimed to have actually visited Crockerland, saying that "here there were musk-oxen, bears, and birds which we shot and ate." Seven years later his story was denied by two American explorers, Professor Donald B. MacMillan and Lieutenant Fitzhugh Green, who found nothing but pack ice when they sledged through the region where Crockerland was supposed to be. "Yet upon our return," Green asserted, "we too saw a land, or something so like land, that had we not been out there we too should have come back certain of its existence."

A decade later aircraft would settle for all time the profile of the Arctic. But until then, the Crockerland legend was too attractive to die. "I want to be with the party when they reach the untrod shores of Crocker Land," lamented Matthew Henson in New York City in 1910; "the lure of the Arctic is tugging at my heart." Said Green, "Land has been seen. Cold could not mar the dream. Volcanic ashes have fallen in Greenland; the Aleutians are buried furnaces. If there be an ice-cooled desert, why not a steam-heated polar paradise?" "The possibility is there," mused Peary. "An isolated island continent, an Arctic Atlantis, with a fauna and flora of its own, as completely isolated from the world as if it were on Mars. Believe me, there is room yet in this prosaic world for a new sensation."

▶▶▶ *Umanak Harbor, northeast Greenland; September 1896. Admiral Robert E. Peary, photographer. Beyond the rocks in the foreground are six kayaks. In 1578 Martin Frobisher "perceived a number of small things fleeting in the sea afarre off, whyche hee supposed to be porposes or seales, or some kind of strange fishe; but on coming nearer, he discovered them to be men in small boates made of leather." Photograph © National Geographic Society. Courtesy of Commander E. P. Stafford.*

THE CONGO

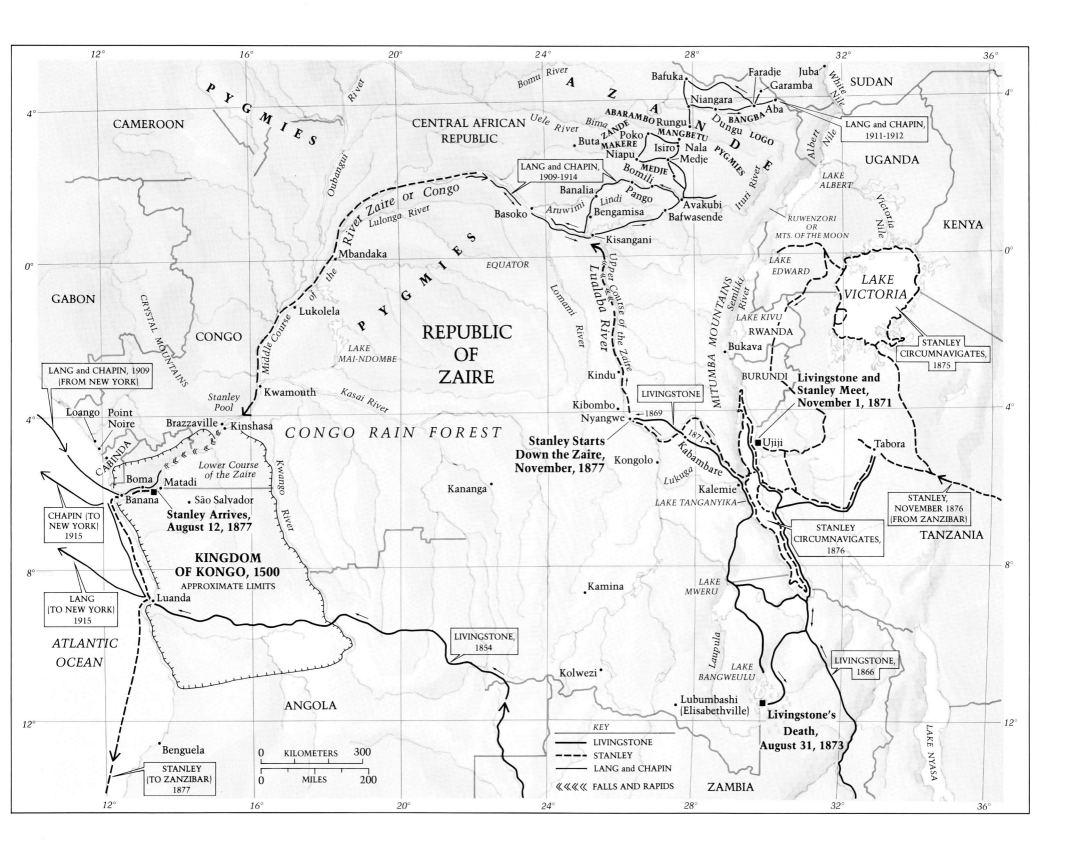

12°　　　　　　　16°　　　　　　　20°　　　　　　　24°　　　　　　　28°　　　　　　　32°　　　　　　　36°

Bomu River

PYGMIES

A Z A N D E

Bafuka　　Faradje　Juba
Niangara　Garamba　White Nile
Aba
SUDAN

CAMEROON

CENTRAL AFRICAN
REPUBLIC

Uele River

Bima　ABARAMBO　Rungu
ZANDE　Poko　MANGBETU　Dungu　LOGO
Buta　MAKERE　Isiro　Nala
Niapu　MEDJE
Medje　PYGMIES

LANG and CHAPIN,
1911-1912

Albert Nile

UGANDA

PYGMIES

Oubangui River

LANG and CHAPIN,
1909-1914

Banalia　Bomili
Pango
Avakubi
Basoko　Bengamisa　Bafwasende
Aruwimi　Lindi
Kisangani

River Zaire or Congo
Lulonga River

LAKE
ALBERT

KENYA

Ituri River

RUWENZORI
OR
MTS. OF THE MOON

0°

Mbandaka

EQUATOR

Lukolela

Lomami River

Upper Course of the Zaire
Lualaba River

LAKE
EDWARD

Victoria Nile

GABON

CRYSTAL MOUNTAINS

PYGMIES

REPUBLIC
OF
ZAIRE

LAKE
MAI-NDOMBE

Middle Course of the Zaire

CONGO

LAKE KIVU
RWANDA
Bukava
BURUNDI

MITUMBA MOUNTAINS
Semliki River

LAKE
VICTORIA

STANLEY
CIRCUMNAVIGATES,
1875

LANG and CHAPIN, 1909
(FROM NEW YORK)

Kwamouth

Kasai River

Kindu

LIVINGSTONE

Livingstone and
Stanley Meet,
November 1, 1871

Loango Point
Noire

Stanley
Pool

Brazzaville　Kinshasa

CONGO RAIN FOREST

Kibombo
Nyangwe　1869
Kongolo

Kabambare
1871
Lukuga

Ujiji

Tabora

Stanley Starts
Down the Zaire,
November, 1877

CABINDA

Boma　Matadi
Banana

Lower Course
of the Zaire

São Salvador

**Stanley Arrives,
August 12, 1877**

Kwango River

Kananga

Kongolo

Kalemie
LAKE TANGANYIKA

STANLEY,
NOVEMBER 1876
(FROM ZANZIBAR)

STANLEY
CIRCUMNAVIGATES,
1876

TANZANIA

CHAPIN (TO
NEW YORK)
1915

**KINGDOM
OF KONGO, 1500**
APPROXIMATE LIMITS

Kamina

*LAKE
MWERU*

LANG
(TO NEW YORK)
1915

Luanda

Kamina

*LAKE
BANGWEULU*

LIVINGSTONE,
1866

*ATLANTIC
OCEAN*

LIVINGSTONE,
1854

Kolwezi

Lubumbashi
(Elisabethville)

**Livingstone's
Death,
August 31, 1873**

STANLEY
(TO ZANZIBAR)
1877

Benguela

ANGOLA

0　　KILOMETERS　　300

0　　MILES　　200

KEY
——— LIVINGSTONE
– – – STANLEY
——— LANG and CHAPIN
«««« FALLS AND RAPIDS

ZAMBIA

*LAKE
NYASA*

12°　　　　　　　16°　　　　　　　20°　　　　　　　24°　　　　　　　28°　　　　　　　32°

While looking at the pictures, get into a Turkish bath.
You will understand the country better.

—Herbert Lang, 1915

In 1909, a pair of American scientists, Herbert Lang and James Chapin, went to the Congo to gather specimens of wildlife for the American Museum of Natural History. They were told to collect everything in "one to three years" and then to return. Five years later, when World War I stopped their work, Lang and Chapin were still there, finding animals unknown to science.

The Congo rain forest is drained by the river Zaire. The Portuguese mariner Diogo Cão was the first European to see the river. In 1482, he sailed into its mouth, where he found a civilized nation called Kongo, several times more populous than his own.

Beyond the mouth of the Zaire, the Congo was unexplored until 1877. In that year, Henry Morton Stanley, a Welsh-born newspaperman, passed through it when he followed the Zaire from its headwaters to the sea. "Imagine the whole of France and the Iberian peninsula closely packed with trees whose crowns of foliage interlace and prevent any view of sky and sun," wrote Stanley. "Then from tree to tree run cables two inches to fifteen inches in diameter, up and down in loops and festoons and W's. Fold them around the trees in great tight coils. Then from the highest branches let fall the ends of the cables reaching near to the ground by hundreds. Work others through and through as confusedly as possible." Imagine this, he wrote, and you will begin to have a mental picture of the Congo rain forest.

After Stanley's visit, the Belgians administered the Congo and oversaw the building of the first roads through the rain forest. Most of these roads, like the one pictured here, were maintained "for security purposes," noted Chapin, but in his time "they had never felt a cart over them."

▸▸▸ *'Typical forest.' Road near Isiro, Province Haut-Zaïre, Republic of Zaire (formerly the Belgian Congo); July 1913. The white man rides a donkey, a mark of distinction; because of the tsetse fly, few draft animals could be kept in the Congo rain forest. Photograph courtesy of The American Museum of Natural History.*

Out of Africa there is always something new.

—Aristotle, *Historia Animalium,* fourth century B.C.

Lang, a German-born zoologist, was twenty-nine when he went to the Congo. "He was a human dynamo," wrote Chapin. "He never hesitated to stay up a whole night developing photographs under the most primitive conditions. He would tramp many miles at night over foot paths in the African forest to make sure he lost not an hour in reaching some creature that had been shot or trapped far away." "K'toto Na Langi"—"Lang's son," as the Congo people called Chapin—was nineteen years old and already a noted ornithologist when he left Columbia University in his junior year to act as Lang's assistant.

"Lang and I were to collect animals from worms and insects up to elephants, prepared in ways suitable for scientific study," Chapin explained. They shot rhinoceros and antelope, poisoned large cats, and caught bats in rat traps baited with guavas. "We killed comparatively few of the animals in our collection," Chapin wrote. "They were killed by the natives for food, and they gave us the skin and skeleton." One man gave them a civet cat that he had clubbed to death in the night as it was dragging a dog from his hut. A Pygmy brought in a large male leopard that he had shot in the heart with a single poisoned arrow. A chief presented them with the skin from the four legs of an okapi; "each one of these, he says, is sufficient to buy a wife," noted Chapin. Birds, which the local people caught in snares or spring traps, or shot with arrows, were purchased with fishhooks, gilt tacks, and salt pills. Chapin habitually

checked hats for feathers that might lead to new species of birds. He kept one such feather for twenty-three years before discovering a new kind of peacock to which it belonged.

Men hired by Chapin once cut down a giant tree to get the hollow section containing a bird's nest. Planning to reconstruct the nest at the Museum, Chapin had the section removed and split into loads for fifteen porters. "The chief of the nearest village paid us a visit, fearing that we intended to gather a medicine of remarkable potency from the nest," Chapin recalled. "But, on seeing the porters shouldering their burdens, 'mere pieces of firewood,' his countenance immediately brightened and he told us that such trees, not hollow, however, and of better wood, were growing right near his village. If we would give him plenty of cloth, copper, brass rings, beads, and salt, he would have as many cut as he had fingers on his hand, and his people would bring them to the post. The white man would never need to come into the wilderness."

➤➤➤ *Two Pygmy chiefs with dead leopard* (Felis panthera pardus), *Gamangui, northeast Zaire; February 1910. Herbert Lang, photographer. Lang entered in his field notes: "The leopard was shot by a pygmy with a single arrow that entered the heart and poisoned as it was, stopped the animal at once." Elsewhere Lang noted that this leopard had "brought grief upon the village by killing the Chief's daughter," and that the hunter had "surprised it while sleeping." Photograph courtesy of The American Museum of Natural History.*

An empty stream, a great silence, an impenetrable forest.

—Joseph Conrad, 1902

To the east of the Congo rain forest are the savannas where several million years ago certain apes first began to evolve into humans. To the north are the savannas where one of the world's early farming civilizations arose. Yet within the forest itself people have never lived in any numbers. "Lean but your hand on a tree, measure but your length on the ground, seat yourself on a fallen branch, and you will then understand what venom and activity breathe around you," Stanley wrote after he marched across the same districts that Lang and Chapin were to cover. "Open your notebook, the page attracts a dozen butterflies, a honey-bee hovers over your hand; other forms of bees dash for your eyes; a wasp buzzes in your ear, a huge hornet menaces your face, an army of ants come marching to your feet."

The Congo is so wet that most of the tribes have rituals to drive away rain. Stanley complained that every mile or so there were "muddy streams, stagnant creeks, and shallow pools, green with duckweed, leaves of lotus and lilies, and a greasy green scum." "Rainstorms of indescribable violence sweep across the country almost every day," reported Chapin. "When rain fell," Stanley said, "no voice could be heard in the camp, the sound of moving branches during a storm was like the roar of breakers." Often, he said, "in the dead of night a series of explosions would wake everyone." First would come a "startling crackle, like a fusillade of musketry, then rending and rushing, ending with a sound that shook the earth." Huge forest trees would be falling.

Falling branches are the "second most frequent cause of death" among the Congo Pygmies, asserted Patrick Putnam, an American who ran a hospital among them for over twenty years. "As the pygmy camp is always constructed in the primary forest itself, never in a clearing, a branch falling in a windstorm may hit a house, killing four or five people at once." The only thing that killed more Pygmies, said Putnam, was falling from trees.

▶▶▶ *'Bridge over the Bima River.' Northeast Zaire; January 1914. Herbert Lang, photographer. Chapin noted that one characteristic of the Congo rain forest is "the diversity of its larger trees," in contrast to northern forests, where stands of one species are common. "But in spite of its luxuriant diversity of forms, the flora of the rain forest in its general composition is fundamentally the same over its entire extent." Photograph courtesy of The American Museum of Natural History.*

We raised our eyes and saw that what we took for a cloud was a bird of enormous size, and it was his wings that darkened the day.

—Sinbad

"Lang and I had already spent about six months in the rain forest," wrote Chapin, "when one day we observed a gigantic bird-claw strung on a woman's necklace." It came from the largest bird of prey in Africa, the crowned eagle, which feeds on monkeys and small antelopes. A friendly local chief eventually announced that one of his men had located a nest. He sent Chapin to a tiny village of "some Walabi who specialized in drop-spears for elephants. Early next morning we stood beneath a gigantic tree in the forest, somewhat isolated from all its neighbors, bearing the eagle's nest. I judged the nest to measure six feet, if not more, across the top. The distance above the ground was about thirty-five yards. There was a young eagle at the nest.

"I spent most of the next three days watching the nest. I sat on the ground in an elephant path at a spot offering a view through the foliage up to the nest. The first day nothing happened till nightfall sent us stumbling back over roots and rivulets by candlelight to our lodging in the forest hamlet.

"The whole of the following day was spent beneath the nest. Only once, toward eleven o'clock, did an old bird visit it. It happened on this day that just while I was examining the ground at the base of the tree [for bones of previous victims], an old eagle had come and gone. Its flight was so noiseless as to escape my ear.

"Arriving at 6:30 on the third morning, we found the young eagle alone on the nest, eating. The third day was running its course. At about four o'clock I was aroused by the eaglet raising its voice excitedly, and jumped to my feet. The old bird had already reached the nest with the foreleg of a monkey. A glance through the glass showed me the adult, with tail turned toward me on the rim of the nest, taking a good look at me over its shoulder. My gazing was finished, and the muzzle of a Winchester returned the bird's stare. My shot dropped the old eagle right on the nest. The young bird took its departure and was not seen again."

The next day it took two men four hours to climb the smooth bole of the great tree and retrieve the dead eagle, "an old female with a spread of some seventy inches, despite the relatively short, rounded form of the wings. We had not been the first to shoot at a bird on this nest. One of the climbers pulled an old arrow out of the bottom of it."

▸▸▸ *'Makere man with crowned eagle* (Stephanoaetus coronatus), *near Niapu.' Northeast Zaire; January 1914. Herbert Lang, photographer. "Several times I have been startled in the forest by the sudden cry of anguish of a monkey who had been seized by this 'leopard of the air,' as the natives call it," related the nineteenth-century American explorer Paul Du Chaillu. Photograph courtesy of The American Museum of Natural History.*

A sound . . . perhaps with as profound
a meaning as the sound of bells in a Christian country.

—Joseph Conrad, 1902

"Drum messages: they are uncanny," wrote a British army officer after he came back from Africa. "When our column was cut up in 1903 I was in [headquarters]. We heard of it two days before the news came through on the telegraph, our source being a native chief who said it had come 'by drum.' "

"The drum message begins with a signal to listen, and then the 'call name' of the person addressed," explained Chapin. He knew drummers with the call names "Pull My Tooth" and "If a Man Hasn't a Wife, I'll Give Him a Wife." Next came the code phrases, "each followed by a short pause, and usually repeated once again to make sure of proper reception. Then a long roll of the drum, gradually dying away, to signify that the message is ended."

A missionary on the middle Zaire River "told of a boy [waiting on table] who was coming into the house with the noonday meal. Just outside the door he stopped, saying he heard a drum-message coming from across the river, seven miles away." The missionary could hear nothing. "The boy waited a while, and then announced that some hunters who had crossed the river had killed two elephants and would be back the next evening. This turned out to be true."

One evening in the forest northwest of the Zaire, an American scientist "was watching a dance, when a drum was heard sending a message from a village about four miles away." He asked a woman what it was saying. "She said that the people of that village had wounded a red pig, and were asking a chief in a third village to bring his dogs the following morning so the pig could be followed and killed. The part of the message that signified 'dog' sounded strangely like the yapping of a dog."

▸▸▸ *Village near Rungu, northeast Zaire; July 1913. Herbert Lang, photographer. Along the upper Zaire River, "every village had its signal drum," noted Chapin. The signal drum shown here is similar in size and shape to one Lang and Chapin brought back for the Museum. A missionary on the middle Zaire reported seeing a drum ten feet high that was reached by a ladder. Photograph courtesy of The American Museum of Natural History.*

The forest is a father and a mother to us. It gives us everything we need.

—Ituri Pygmy, ca. 1956

An inscription from a tomb near Aswan contains instructions from the pharaoh Neferkare, who ruled in the twenty-eighth century B.C., to a merchant who was to journey up the Nile through the Sudan towards the Congo: "Thou shalt bring this dwarf with thee, living and healthy from the land of spirits to rejoice and gladden the heart of the king of Upper and Lower Egypt."

The ancient Mediterranean peoples knew about the Pygmies, but it was not until after the Portuguese discoveries in Guinea and Kongo that modern Europeans began to believe reports of a people the size of children living in the forests of central Africa. A seventeenth-century Dutch explorer, Olfert Dapper, wrote that the king of Loango, a country on the African coast above the Zaire, was "attended by dwarf pages, and the black men said that a certain wilderness was inhabited exclusively by dwarfs like these, who were wont to kill considerable numbers of elephants." Pygmies were first brought to Europe in 1867 by an Italian expedition that had crossed into the northeast Congo from the Nile watershed and returned with two boys. The count of Verona taught the pair to read and write Italian.

The traditions of the peoples native to the Congo rain forest all agree that the Pygmies were the first to live there. The Pygmies' smaller size is probably a favorable adaptation for moving in the dense undergrowth, and the lighter shade of their skin may be an adaptation related to the lack of sunlight beneath the forest canopy.

The Pygmies live in temporary camps under the trees in the virgin forest. Most of the other peoples live in permanent villages in clearings. The Pygmies hunt; the others farm and fish. The Pygmies know the medicinal and edible plants in their territories; the others rarely do.

Today, as in Lang and Chapin's time, the Pygmies are greatly outnumbered by their taller, darker neighbors. But it is the Pygmies who are, as they themselves say, "the people of the forest." The other groups generally avoid going into the deep jungle. Instead, they have Pygmy intermediaries with whom they trade their cultivated foods for forest products, such as meat and honey. To them the forest is something evil that must be cut back when it intrudes on their clearings. But to the Pygmies, the jungle is something good, from which life comes. "The forest," they say, "is our home. When the forest dies, we shall die."

➤➤➤ *Pygmy village near Nala, northeast Zaire; July 1913. Herbert Lang, photographer. Lang made plaster of Paris casts of the Pygmies' faces. They were usually frightened when he covered them with the "soft white mud," Chapin noted, but "Emandinia, chief of the Nala Pygmies, exhibited complete calm while having his cast taken, saying 'Were not the white men alone, and Emandinia supported by 100 well-trained archers?'" Photograph courtesy of The American Museum of Natural History.*

God gave it to us. He said to the old beast, "Go up there;
men are come who will kill and eat you."

—Tribal elephant hunter, 1855

The Pygmies hunt elephants alone. "Not every pygmy has the courage to face an elephant and kill it," wrote Patrick Putnam, "and not every man the skill. His technique of hunting is daring and simple." The Pygmy uses a special spear with a short handle and a long thin blade. "Before approaching his quarry," wrote the anthropologist Jean Janmart, "the pygmy hunter goes to one of the shallow pools, where the animals have their daily mudbath, and smears his entire body with mud, so he cannot be smelled out by his quarry. He is absolutely naked when hunting."

Then, Putnam continued, "he tracks the elephant until he sees it through the underbrush. He approaches silently, up wind; he jabs his spear as far as he can into the elephant, gashing the belly just behind the ribs; then he pulls it right out again. The elephant at this point usually turns, and the pygmies say that if you as much as wink at this moment you are dead.

"The man stands stock still, so the elephant can't see him. Then he goes through a sequence of stab and jump and stand still, as many times as he can. Every time the elephant looks away he stabs him, and every time the elephant turns he stands still. The elephant can run faster than a man, and the pygmy's only hope is to wound the animal so badly that it will be unable to catch him before he gets away.

"Finally the elephant goes charging off with one or more wounds in his intestines. The hunter, with his spear in his hand, returns to the camp. There is much excitement; men, women, and children crowd around him and inspect the spear. If it is bloody way down to such and such a point, then the elephant has a serious wound and they will follow him until he finally lies down and dies of peritonitis."

▸▸▸ *'Male elephant, view of entire specimen.' Near Faradje, northeast Zaire; ca. 1911. Herbert Lang, photographer. The largest African elephant* (Loxodonta africana) *ever recorded was 13 feet, 2 inches tall at the shoulder (Smithsonian Institution). The largest Asiatic elephant* (Elephas indicus) *was 10 feet, 8 inches tall (Rowland Ward). The largest fossil elephant was the imperial mammoth* (Archidiskidon imperator), *which lived in the southern United States when humans first arrived there and was about 14 feet tall. Photograph courtesy of The American Museum of Natural History.*

I brought down ten immense bull elephants on the banks of the Haber.

—Tomb inscription of Assyrian king, twelfth century B.C.

The neighboring forests swarm with every kind of elephant.

—Roman soldier, first century A.D.

During the hunting, will we catch elephants or not?

—Oracle bone inscription, Shang Dynasty, fourteenth century B.C.

The Assyrian king hunted along the banks of the Khabur River in northeastern Syria; the Roman soldier was describing the Atlas Mountains in North Africa; the oracle bone was found in An-yang, North China. Wild elephants do not live near any of these places today. But when men and women first lived in Europe, Asia, and Africa, elephants were to be found in almost every part of those continents. When *Homo sapiens* reached the Americas, proboscideans were there too.

Most of the elephants have vanished since the end of the last ice age. Changing climates, flooded plains, and long droughts killed many; epidemics probably wiped out others. But this cannot explain how so many other types of animals subject to the same conditions could have survived while the members of the Proboscidean Order, which inhabited nearly the whole of the earth, fed on a wide array of plants still existing today, were so powerful that they had few predators, had a greater ability to grasp and manipulate than almost any other quadruped, and had the largest brain of any land animal, should have vanished completely on three of the continents they inhabited and retreated to a fraction of their former range on the other two.

It is likely that man was the chief cause of their extinction. While the elephants were evolving towards greater body size, man was evolving towards greater brain size. Man, with no particular physical advantage over other beasts, became a group hunter, and since to the hunter large game is always preferable to small, the conspicuous proboscideans were among man's chief prey.

On every continent where elephants lived, sites have been found where their bones lie mixed together with stone tools. A Stone Age camp at Předmost, Czechoslovakia, yielded the skeletons of six hundred woolly mammoths, mostly juveniles. At another Stone Age site their bones were stacked in piles, "each kind of bone to its own heap." In classical times tribes of Elephantophagi—elephant eaters—were known of in places where elephants do not live today. And before Europeans came to the African forests in search of ivory, elephants were hunted there routinely for food, and their tusks were used incidentally for fences, doorposts, and implements such as log wedges, hammer heads, and horns, just as they had been ten thousand years earlier in Eurasia and America.

➤➤ *'Caravan from Haut Ituri with ivory. 97 tusks in all. On right in picture is 221cm tusk [7 feet, 3 inches].' Avakubi, northeast Zaire; November 1909. Herbert Lang, photographer. The largest known tusk from an African elephant is 11 feet, 5½ inches long and weighs 235 pounds. This record is from an elephant killed in the nineteenth century. Few today are left alive whose tusks are more than one-quarter that size. Photograph courtesy of The American Museum of Natural History.*

There lies the Kongo Kingdom, great and strong,
Already led by us to Christian ways.

—Luis de Camoës, *The Lusiads* 5. 13 (1572)

On a fall day in 1482 Portuguese mariners sailed into the mouth of the Zaire River. They were greeted by the citizens of Kongo, and two worlds met. The Kongolese had never seen or heard of white men before. And the Portuguese had made the first European contact with a civilization south of the equator.

The Kingdom of Kongo stretched along three hundred miles of coast south of the Zaire and extended about two hundred miles inland to the Kwango River. Its several million inhabitants cultivated sorghum, millet, bananas, and oil palms; kept pigs, goats, and poultry; smelted copper and iron; and wove a fine cloth from the raffia palm. They did not make use of writing, the wheel, or the calendar. A hereditary king sat in an elaborate court attended by several hundred wives and a greater number of nobles. He could raise an army of a hundred thousand warriors in a few days.

The king of Kongo saw that the superior arts and arms of the new arrivals might be used to advance the power of his nation. At first he welcomed the priests and soldiers that were sent by the Portuguese, but soon he began to fear their strength. After a few years he banished them to a distant province of his realm, along with their chief supporter, his son and heir Affonso.

During his exile Affonso surrounded himself with Portuguese tutors and studied every aspect of European culture. When he ascended the throne of Kongo at the death of his father in 1506, he brought back the Portuguese. They helped him build a capital in European style called São Salvador, which in time covered twenty square miles and held a hundred thousand people. The nobles of his court dressed "according to the Portuguese fashion, wearing cloaks, capes, scarlet tabards, and silk robes, everyone according to his means," wrote the Portuguese chronicler Lopes. Affonso sent hundreds of students, including the heir to the throne, to Lisbon to be educated. In Rome, one of his sons was made a bishop by Pope Leo X.

►►► *'Queen Mutubani of the Mangbetu Tribe, painted by her servants.' Okondo's town, northeast Zaire; December 1910. Herbert Lang, photographer. Mutubani was Okondo's principal wife. According to Lang she was then over sixty, had borne nearly a score of children, and had survived three husbands. She was still alive when Okondo died in 1916. Photograph courtesy of The American Museum of Natural History.*

[The son of a Kongolese chief was entrusted] when eight or ten years old, to a Liverpool captain to learn to "make book" in England; his guardian found it less troublesome to have him taught to make sugar in St. Kitts, where he accordingly sold him.

—Captain James Tuckey, 1816

The Portuguese that the old king had driven from Kongo owned little territory outside Europe. The Portuguese that returned with Affonso ten years later were the masters of Brazil, and that virgin expanse needed labor to make its masters rich. When the Portuguese asked to buy slaves, at first Affonso obliged, as his father had done, by selling the criminals of his realm. But a whole continent was waiting to be settled, and there were not enough wrongdoers in all of Africa to fill the plantations of Brazil. When Affonso ran out of criminals, Portuguese agents fomented crime and rebellion to make more. They raided and kidnapped. They even enslaved some of Affonso's grandchildren, whom he had entrusted to them to educate in Europe.

The people of Kongo resisted the slavers locally. Near the end of Affonso's reign the Portuguese quarter of São Salvador was burned. But Affonso avoided a war that he knew he could not win, and instead sent envoys to Rome to plead for Christian restraint. He died in 1545. In the following century, Kongo was beset by famine, plague, civil war, and invaders from other parts of Africa as well as Europe. The succeeding kings set up their own slave stations and competed with the Portuguese.

In 1641 the Kongolese allied themselves with the Dutch and drove the Portuguese from their country. Seven years later the Portuguese forced their way back. In 1665 they crushed the Kongolese army in a great battle and beheaded the king. The Kongo state rapidly disintegrated, and from then on the only rulers were petty chiefs, and the slavers prowled freely through the land.

The Belgian missionaries reported that when they arrived in São Salvador at the end of the nineteenth century, four hundred years after the first Portuguese, they found "only a few vestiges of Christianity: some rites that had lost their meaning, here and there a church wall leveled with the ground and covered with grass, and some copper crucifixes, made in the region, that had been preserved for generations."

▶▶ *'Mondo man of Maruka's people—all apparel in collection.' Witch doctor, Logo tribe; Gambara, northeast Zaire; June 1912. Herbert Lang, photographer. At the witch doctor's feet are his tools: whistles for killing thieves or making women fertile, a stone with a hole in it used for telling fortunes, horns and tusks for giving the bearer the traits of the animals they come from. Photograph courtesy of The American Museum of Natural History.*

According to an old chronicle, Beatrice had fine features and a tall slender form. She spoke with gravity, appearing to weigh each word, and her outward manner was devout. She was about twenty-two years old when she was burned to death in Kongo on July 2, 1706.

Her home was at the foot of the hills where a young heir to the Kongo throne, Pedro IV, had been driven by his enemies. In her youth she had learned about fetishes from the native priests, and about Christianity from the European missionaries. As she grew older, she had dreams and visions and began to predict the future. Several times she lay down as if dead and rose again after seven days. She announced that Anthony, the patron saint of Portugal, had entered her head. Taking his name and donning a crown of bark, Beatrice went out to preach to the people of Kongo. She proclaimed that they must destroy all crosses and images of Christ, and bar all foreign missionaries from Kongo. Henceforth, the falling rain would be enough to wash away their sins, and men could again take more than one wife, as they had done in the past. From every part of the country great multitudes calling themselves Antonians gathered around her.

To young King Pedro, Beatrice promised that she would restore the monarchy, which was then split into several factions. She went to his chief rival, King João, who wore the crown of Kongo, and demanded that he surrender it to Pedro. But João drove her away, saying that if Pedro believed in her, he was a child who was not worthy to be king.

Having failed in her mission, Beatrice dared not return to Pedro. Instead she preached that God was angered by the rivalry between the two kings, and called on her followers to choose a new one. Pedro and João both vowed to destroy her for this, and she fled into the bush. There she bore a male child.

But Pedro's soldiers found her and brought her to him. His judges, urged on by the missionaries, condemned her to be burned. When she heard the sentence, she replied, "What does it matter to me to die? My body could come to no other end. It is only a bit of earth." Some of her enemies wanted to burn her child with her, but he was taken off to be raised by the missionaries.

On the day of her execution, Beatrice was led to a large square. She was bound, and wore her bark crown. A great multitude had assembled there. Her sentence was read by a judge dressed from head to foot in black, "black so ugly that one could never find another to rival its ugliness," wrote a priest. Then Beatrice was thrown onto a great pile of wood and burned. The next day her remains were burned again, until nothing was left but the finest ash. Years later, a Portuguese missionary reported that "at the present, in order that she may be forgotten, it is still necessary to avoid any mention of the name Saint Anthony."

▸▸▸ *'Medje woman and child. Child's head bound. Woman wears banana leaves.' Town of Medje, northeast Zaire; September 1910. Herbert Lang, photographer. The Mangbetu tribe, to which the Medje are related, are famous for binding the heads of their infants of both sexes. Chapin claimed it did not affect their brains, which were "as good as my own." Photograph courtesy of The American Museum of Natural History.*

The river that swallows all rivers.

—Kongo tribe's name for the Zaire River

Ever since Diogo Cão discovered the mouth of the Zaire in 1482, Europeans had known where the river ended, but not where it came from. Stirred by hopes that it might lead them across Africa to the Indies, the Portuguese tried to ascend the Zaire. Cão sailed up the river until he was stopped by the lowest set of rapids, about fifty miles from the coast. In 1491, the people of Kongo led Portuguese soldiers two hundred miles inland to the great pool above the rapids. Then in 1497 the Portuguese rounded the Cape of Good Hope and opened a sea route to the Indies—to their "unspeakable gaine," wrote an English rival. Thereafter they no longer bothered with a route through the interior of Africa, and the course of the Zaire remained unknown until Stanley traced it in 1877.

The Zaire crosses the equator twice: first where it drops into a basin nine hundred miles across that contains the Congo rain forest, and again where it spills out of this basin, after having gathered more water than any river except the Amazon. Then it rushes through a gorge, forming the greatest rapids on earth, and flows into the Atlantic. One stretch of these rapids, four miles long and half a mile broad, reminded Stanley of "a strip of sea blown over by a hurricane,"

with waves thirty feet high, whirlpools that could draw under a large boat, and a roar so deafening that it benumbed.

In the four centuries between Cão and Stanley, the only major attempt to explore the river was made by the British Admiralty. In 1816, noting that it was "incompatible with the present advanced state of geographical science that a river of such magnitude as the Zaire should not be known with any degree of certainty, beyond, if so far as, 200 miles from its mouth," they sent Captain James Tuckey upriver with a party of thirty-eight men equipped with portable boats. Six weeks later the party returned. Twenty-one had died, "and though the greater number were carried off by a most violent fever," reported a doctor who was with the expedition, "some of them appeared to have no ailment and actually to have died from exhaustion."

►►► *'Middle Zaire River at Maberu, just above Lukolela. Natives in a large dugout canoe.' Northwest Zaire; October 1930. James P. Chapin, photographer. The river averages about four miles in width over its middle course and swells in places to twenty miles, but it contracts to a few hundred yards in the gorges of its lower course. Photograph courtesy of The American Museum of Natural History.*

You are bad, you have not wings, the river is deep. Go back.

—River inhabitants to Stanley's party, 1876

By following Arab slavers inland from the east coast of Africa, the Scottish explorer Dr. David Livingstone reached the banks of a large river called the Lualaba in 1871. He hoped it was the Nile. Neither the slavers nor the local people knew where it went. Livingstone wanted to follow it, but he lost his way in the swamps near its source and died of dysentery. Before he died, he met Stanley and told him about the river.

Stanley was determined to take up where Livingstone had left off. By November of 1876, he had reached the Lualaba. He asked the slaver who had been farthest down-river where it flowed.

"It flows north."

"And then?"

"It flows north!"

"And then?"

"Still north!"

"Come, my friend, speak, whither does it flow after reaching the north?"

With "a broad smile of wonder" at Stanley's "apparent lack of ready comprehension," the slaver replied:

"Why, master, don't I tell you it flows north, and north, and north, and there is no end to it."

From this Stanley concluded that "the great problem of African geography was left untouched at the exact spot where Dr. Livingstone had been unable to prosecute his travels."

Stanley set off down the river in a score of stolen dugout canoes with 143 part-black Zanzibar Arabs (the survivors of 230 who had accompanied him from the east coast) and one white (out of the three who had been with him at the start). The river flowed through a vast rain forest. Its banks were thinly inhabited by tribes of fishermen and farmers. Each tribe controlled a stretch of water and defended it from any intruders. "Go back!" they shouted at Stanley.

"But we are doing no harm, friends. It is the river that takes us down, and the river will not stop, or go back."

"This is our river."

"Good. Tell it to take us back, and we will go."

"If you do not go back, we will fight you."

But the tribes on the upper Zaire knew better than to attack. They were armed with spears and bows. Stanley had guns, and these tribes had already learned that "the gun is the sultan of Africa."

▸▸▸ 'Reception for Chief Maruka. Maruka at left, Kasima at right.' Two chiefs, Logo tribe, near Faradje, northeast Zaire; July 1911. Herbert Lang, photographer. Both chiefs, noted Lang, had helped the Belgians drive Sudanese rebels out of the northeast Congo in 1897. Photograph courtesy of The American Museum of Natural History.

The gun is the sultan of Africa.

—Saying among nineteenth-century Zanzibar slavers

The people living along the upper course of the Zaire had learned about guns from Arab slavers. On the lower Zaire they knew about guns from European slavers. But on the middle Zaire, where no outsiders had been, the people had never seen firearms. They attacked Stanley's party thirty-two times as it floated through their waters. Stanley described one fight: "Looking upstream, we see a flotilla of gigantic canoes bearing down upon us. We form a line. I give the order to drop anchor. Four of our canoes affect not to listen, until I chase them and threaten them with my guns. This compelled them to return to the line, which is formed of eleven double canoes, anchored ten yards apart. The shields are next lifted by the non-combattants and from behind these the muskets and rifles are aimed.

"[The warriors] advance to the attack with drums, 100 blasts from ivory horns, and cries. They let fly their spears and there is a noise of rushing bodies. But every sound is soon lost in the ripping, crackling musketry. Some of their men are in the river, others lie in the bottom of canoes, groaning and dying.

"As these retire a magnificent war canoe comes down to reinforce them. It probably is the King's canoe, and contains about 100 men. Six are perched on a platform at the bow, hideously painted and garnished with head-dresses of feathers, while one stalks backwards and forwards with a crown of feathers. There are about sixty paddlers, their bodies bending and swaying in unison, as with a swelling chorus they drive her down towards us. Each paddle is decorated with an ivory ball handle, and the staff is wound about with copper and iron wire. From the bow streams a thick fringe of long white fibre.

"The monster canoe aims straight for my boat, but when fifty yards off, swerves aside. The warriors above the manned prow let fly their spears." But Stanley's guns repelled them. They responded to each successful shot "with wild cries of surprise, rage, and sorrow mixed."

▶▶▶ *'The falls showing the famous native fisheries.' Zaire River at Kisangani (Stanleyville), northeast Zaire; ca. August 1909. Herbert Lang, photographer. "At the foot of the falls are long conical fish-traps attached by vines to the wooden framework," Chapin wrote. The falls divide the upper from the middle Zaire. It was near here that Stanley was first attacked. Photograph courtesy of The American Museum of Natural History.*

It is a bad world, master, and you have lost your way in it.

—Dying words of one of Stanley's followers, 1877

"To continue this fearful life was not possible," Stanley wrote after he had been fighting the tribes of the middle Zaire for nearly two months. "There were not thirty in the entire expedition that had not received a wound. Day and night we are pained with the dreadful drumming which announces our arrival and their fears of our purposes. We have no interpreter, and cannot make ourselves understood. We have been unable to purchase food; or indeed approach a settlement for any amicable purpose."

Then one day Stanley's party came upon three natives fishing. "They replied to us clearly and calmly. There was none of that fierce bluster and wild excitement that we had come to recognize as the preliminary symptoms of a conflict. The word ndu—brother—was more frequent." Stanley's party followed them across the river to their village, where they found "four ancient Portuguese muskets, at the sight of which the people of the Expedition raised a glad shout. These appeared to them certain signs that the great river did really reach the sea." When Stanley asked the village chief for the name of the river, "after he had quite comprehended the drift of the question, he replied in a sonorous voice, 'Ikutu ya Kongo!'—the river of Congo-land." For the first time Stanley knew that the river he was following was the Zaire.

Below there the tribes were more friendly, and Stanley's party passed easily to the great rapids near the mouth of the river. But when they tried to descend the rapids, twelve canoes were wrecked and thirteen men were drowned, including the last white besides Stanley. In one thirty-seven-day period, they went thirty-four miles. They finally quit the canoes in the rapids and struck out on foot for the coast. On August 10, 1877, exactly one thousand days after Stanley had left Zanzibar, he and about half of his original party emerged at the mouth of the Zaire on the other side of Africa.

▸▸▸ *The twelve wives of [Chief] Kasima' (of the Logo tribe). Near Faradje, northeast Zaire; July 1911. Herbert Lang, photographer. Photograph courtesy of The American Museum of Natural History.*

We sacrifice a goat each year to the Spirit of the Falls.
You give nothing; how can you hope to escape?

—Lower Zaire River chief to Stanley, 1877

"Soudi was handsome," wrote Stanley, and "a great favorite of the female wantons" wherever he went. Leaving his native Zanzibar in 1874, Soudi went with Stanley into the Congo, where he saw his brother killed by hostile tribesmen and was himself wounded three times before he was swept over a falls on the lower Zaire in March 28, 1877.

Six men had already been drowned that day. They were in a canoe over eighty-five feet long. The steersman tried to guide it near the shore, but, Stanley related, "the current wafted him slowly into the middle of the mighty river where human strength availed nothing, and the canoe glided by over the treacherous calm surface to doom. Presently we saw the stern pointed upward"—in a whirlpool below the falls.

Another canoe then broke from the people who had been holding it on the bank. No one was in it but Soudi. He knew nothing of steering, wrote Stanley, "but paddled his canoe as if by instinct. As he passed us, he shouted at me, 'I am lost, master; there is but one God.' The river caught him and his canoe in its tremendous force, great waves struck madly at him, and yet his canoe did not sink, but he and it were seen to sweep behind an island and we could see nothing more, for darkness fell on us and on the river."

Three days later he returned, "to our general joy," wrote Stanley. "He had been swept down by the fierce current and whirled round so often that he was almost giddy, then fi-

nally landed far below, just at night, on the summit of a lone rock. He swam ashore and was immediately seized by a man and dragged inland several hours journey in the night. He was taken to a hut and fed, and told to go to sleep, but in the night, Soudi was heard digging his way to freedom and the man bound him.

"Next morning the captor informed his neighbors of the merits of his prize and many came to view Soudi, among whom was a subject of [a king whom Stanley had visited a few days earlier]. The king's subject drew such a terrible picture of a white man with large fiery eyes and long black hair who possessed a little instrument around his waist which killed any number of men at once, that it was a danger to the entire country to detain any of his men. This so frightened [Soudi's captor] that he at once led Soudi to the falls near which he found him. 'Go,' said he, 'to your king, here is food for you until he comes, but do not tell him, I entreat you, that I placed you in bonds. Tell him I fed you and he will be pleased with us.' "

▸▸▸ *Left: 'An Abarambo chief in costume before a dance.' Near Poko, northeast Zaire; August 1913. Herbert Lang, photographer. Right: 'Member of the Bangba tribe wearing hat covered with shells of water snail* (Pila confoensis) *and feathers of the crowned eagle* (Stephanoaetus coronatus). *Near Niapu, northeast Zaire; January 1914. Herbert Lang, photographer. Both photographs courtesy of The American Museum of Natural History.*

We ate meat till our teeth fell out.

—Congo tribesman, telling
Chapin about the feast after a hippopotamus hunt, 1913

"Their chief characteristic is their courage," Livingstone wrote of a tribe of hippopotamus hunters he met while exploring a river south of the Zaire. "They follow no other occupation, but when their game is getting scanty at one spot, they remove to some other part of [the river], and build temporary huts on an island, where their women cultivate patches: the flesh of the animals they kill is eagerly exchanged by the more settled people for grain."

"Their hunting is the bravest thing I ever saw," he continued. "They use long light [canoes] formed for speed. Each canoe is manned by two men. Each man uses a broad short paddle. They guide the canoe slowly down stream to a sleeping Hippopotamus. Not a single ripple is raised on the smooth water. They look as if holding their breath, and communicate by signs only. As they come near the prey the harpooner in the bow lays down his paddle and rises slowly up, and there he stands, erect, motionless, and eager with the long-handled weapon poised at arm's length above his head, til coming close to the beast he plunges it with all his might in towards the heart. During this he has to keep his balance exactly. His neighbor in the stern at once backs his paddle, the harpooner sits down, seizes his paddle, and backs too to escape. The animal, surprised and wounded, [goes underwater and] seldom returns the attack at this stage of the hunt.

"The next stage, however, is full of danger. The barbed blade of the harpoon is secured by a strong rope [to a float]. The hunter hauls on the rope until he knows that he is right over the beast. When he feels the line suddenly slacken he is prepared to deliver another harpoon the instant the hippo's enormous jaws appear above the water. When caught by many harpoons, and weakened by loss of blood, the hippo succumbs.

"But the hippo often assaults the canoe, crunches it with his jaws as easily as a pig would a bunch of asparagus, or shivers it with a kick by his hind foot. Deprived of their canoe the hunters instantly dive and swim to the shore under water: they say that the infuriated beast looks for them on the surface, and being below they escape his sight. The danger may be appreciated if one remembers that no sooner is blood shed in the water than all the crocodiles below are immediately drawn upstream by the scent, and are ready to act the part of thieves in a London crowd, or worse."

▸▸▸ *'Black Forest Pig, male.' Medje, northeast Zaire; ca. 1909. Herbert Lang, photographer.* Hylochoerus meinertzhageni, *the giant forest hog, is also found in the Amazon forests, where it was introduced in early post-Columbian times by the Portuguese or their African slaves. The males are said to charge without provocation. Photograph courtesy of The American Museum of Natural History.*

You eat fowls and goats and we eat men; why not? what is the difference?

—People of the Zaire River to missionaries, end of nineteenth century

In the Congo rain forest, the Pygmies had plenty of meat: the wild game they had long ago learned how to hunt. However, in recent centuries, tall people from the neighboring savannas made their way into the forests. Perhaps they came to escape drought or slave raiders or plague. Out on the plains, they had gotten meat from herds of wild and domestic grazing animals. But grazers will not thrive in the forest, and the arts of hunting forest animals take tribes generations to learn. For food, the plainsmen had to burn away the forest and plant crops in the thin soil. To get meat, many allied themselves to Pygmy bands and traded their crops for wild game. Others learned to fish or hunt on the rivers. And a few preyed on their own kind.

Perhaps they were led to cannibalism by eating the hearts of their fallen enemies, or the hands of chimpanzees, as Livingstone saw people doing on the upper Zaire. In any event, cannibalism became rampant in the nineteenth century as outsiders pushing into the Congo in search of ivory, slaves, and rubber forced the natives to tend to their defense rather than their crops. Hundreds of thousands are supposed to have starved. Often, those who lived did so at the expense of others.

▶▶▶ *Trial of accused cannibals, Avakubi, northeast Zaire; September 29, 1909. Herbert Lang, photographer. At left are the four defendants, who were supposed to have committed ritual murders and cannibalism for the Secret Society of the Leopard. The Leopard men ambushed their victims and killed them with iron claws fastened to their hands. The society was reputed to have an antiforeign purpose, but the victims were always other blacks. There are leopard societies among the forest tribes in both Central and West Africa. In the eastern Congo, over 100 killings had been ascribed to them by 1922, when the Belgians sent an expedition against them. Ten were caught and hanged at that time, but they were rumored to have been innocent "stand-ins." The presiding judge in this photograph, seated beneath his bird specimens, is a Swiss employed by the Congo Free State. At the left of the table is the court interpreter; at the right is the chief of the village where the victims lived and his interpreter. The Belgian Office of African Archives say they have no record of the fate of the accused. Photograph courtesy of The American Museum of Natural History.*

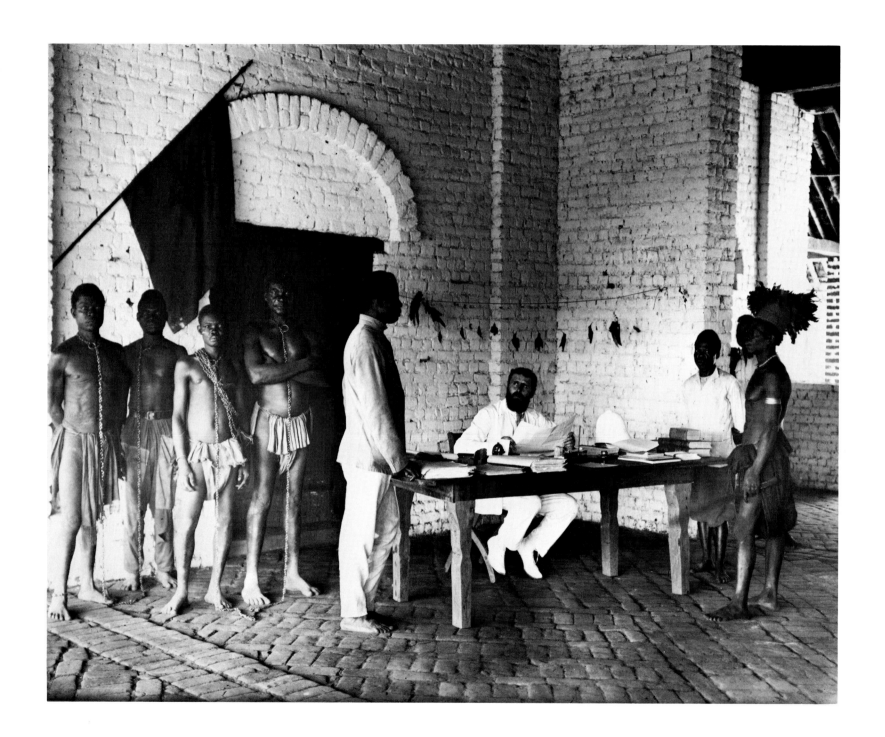

In Equatorial Africa, a small bird called a honey guide (*Indicator indicator*) actually ushers other animals to trees containing honey. "Before the arrival of Europeans," noted Chapin, "an Azande chief would have cut off the ear of any man so stupid as to have killed a honey guide."

Chapin wrote that soon after he arrived in the Congo in 1909, he "began to hear a mysterious, reiterated nasal sound of a tin-horn quality. It seemed to come out of thin air, for no bird could I see that might produce it. I was puzzled by this sound for four years." Chapin found that each tribe "was familiar with the sound and had a name for its author, the Azande calling it *nyete* in imitation of its voice. But whenever you ask them what bird it is, they say, 'the bird is invisible. You can hear it, but you can't see it.' "

In 1913, he continued, "from a high tree not far off the track came a loud note ('cutta cutta'), totally unfamiliar. A glance with the glass revealed a dull colored bird no larger than a starling, but with a tail just like an inverted fleur-de-lis. This one I shot immediately, and a second bird of the same kind took wing and flew off to our right. After I picked up my bird, which proved to be a new honey guide (*Melichneutes robustus*), there came from the sky, off to our right, that mysterious nasal sound. The 'nyete, nyete, nyete' call seemed to be coming toward us, and then it ceased and a second honey guide with the fleur-de-lis tail was seen to alight in another tall tree not far away. On examining the first bird, I found that at each side of the fleur-de-lis tail there were three rather short, stiff, narrow feathers. From what I knew of similar tail-quills of snipe I at once concluded these feathers must vibrate as the bird dove from the sky and produce the nasal noises.

"All this was sufficient to convince me that now we had our invisible bird! There was just one narrow link missing in our chain of evidence. We had not actually seen our bird as it produced its nasal tooting sounds."

Chapin left the Congo before he got a chance to see one of the birds making the noise, and it was not until 1949 that an ornithologist in Cameroon "finally succeeded in observing these honey-guides as they circled silently up to a height of 200 yards over the forest, then came shooting steeply down, opening and shutting their tail and wings, which sets the tail quills to vibrating. The speed of the dive explains readily why the bird is so difficult to sight. If it is 600 feet away, the first 'toots' will require a half-second to reach the watcher's ear. By the time he has focused on the starting point, the bird is perhaps 100 feet away in its downward course, and the more he keeps looking at the point where the noise seemed to begin, the less apt he is to perceive its maker."

▶▶▶ *Rain forest between Bengamisa and Banalia, northeast Zaire; July 1914. Herbert Lang, photographer. A man is standing between the two trees in the foreground, each of which is twice as tall as the portions shown here. Photograph courtesy of The American Museum of Natural History.*

I was mighty fortunate to be able to profit by the best
half century that equatorial Africa ever offered to a naturalist,
when the country was new, yet safe for travel.

—James P. Chapin

News of the outbreak of World War I reached Lang and Chapin three weeks late, at the main Belgian outpost above Stanleyville. Of the eight whites there, Lang and four others were German. "Gentlemen," said the Belgian postmaster, "none of us started this war, and we're all going to be friends as before." Lang was so highly respected by the Belgian administrators in the Congo that they ignored his German nationality and allowed him to sail to the United States. He stayed with the American Museum until 1925 and then moved to Pretoria, South Africa, where he worked at the Transvaal Museum. He died in South Africa in 1957 when he was seventy-eight.

Chapin spent the last two years of the expedition shepherding their collections homeward. He hired over 2,000 bearers to carry everything down to Stanleyville. Lang calculated that he and Chapin had engaged a total of 38,000 bearers while they were in the Congo (in the forest, bearers carried only a few days before returning to their villages) and had themselves "traveled about 15,000 miles on foot without accident or sickness." At Stanleyville, Chapin was to pack everything for shipment to New York by steamer. Thousands of knocked-down crates had been sent out with the expedition. In the five years that these had lain in a warehouse, termites had turned the boards to dust, and the nails had rusted. To get planks, Chapin had trees cut and sawn; for nails, he had dozens of old muskets melted down and hammered out. When the collections were ready to be shipped, they weighed fifty-four tons. There were nearly 25,000 skeletons, skins, and carcasses; 100,000 insects; 10,000 photographs; scores of face casts; and thousands of things made or used by the people of the Congo, including several hundred carved ivory pieces.

Chapin arrived in New York with the collections in March 1915, five years and ten months after he had left home. He was still only twenty-five years old. He worked at the American Museum of Natural History for the rest of his life. His four-volume work on the birds of the Congo took him forty years to complete and is one of the great works of ornithology. He returned to Africa four times before his death in 1964 at the age of seventy-four.

▸▸▸ *Caravan of the Congo expedition of the American Museum, after a twenty-two-day march through the forest. Near Avakubi, northeast Zaire; ca. July 1914. Herbert Lang, photographer. Photograph courtesy of The American Museum of Natural History.*

THE GOBI

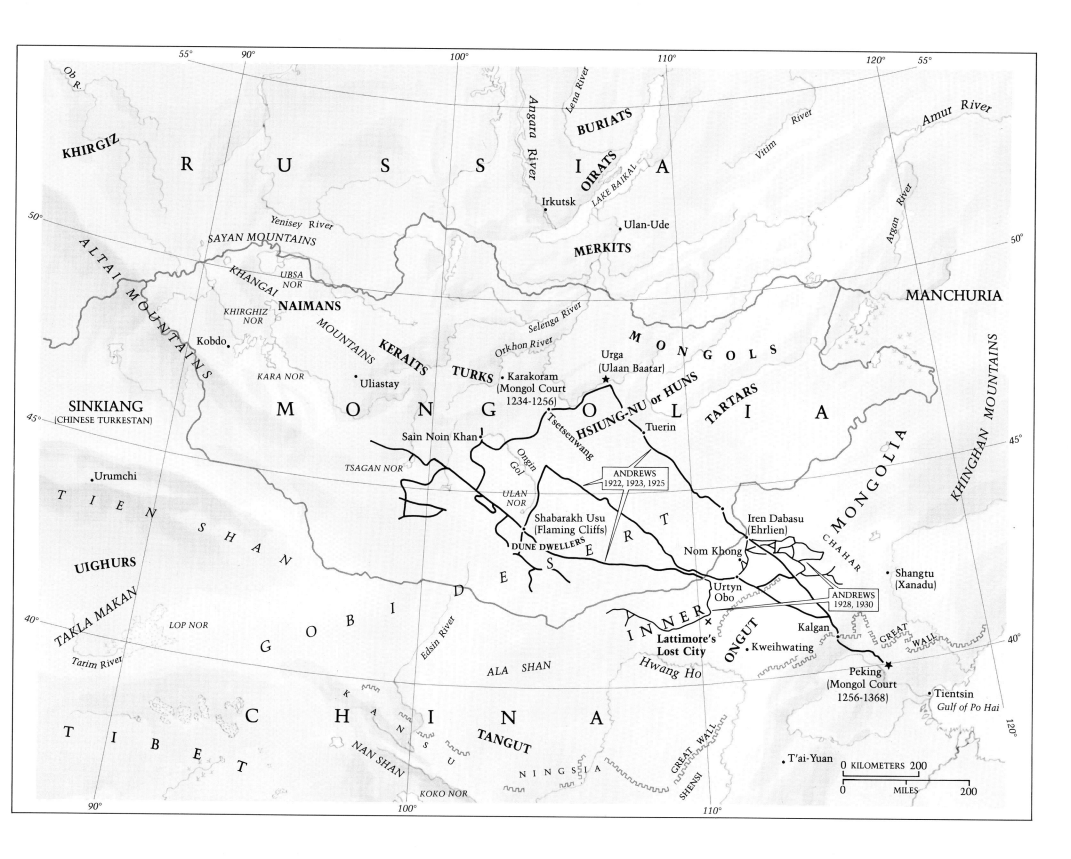

55°   90°   100°   110°   120°   55°

Ob R.

KHIRGIZ

R   U   S   S   I   A

Lena River

BURIATS

Angara River

OIRATS

LAKE BAIKAL

• Irkutsk

• Ulan-Ude

Vitim

River

Amur River

50°   *Yenisey River*   50°

SAYAN MOUNTAINS

MERKITS

ALTAI

KHANGAI

UBSA NOR

NAIMANS

KHIRGHIZ NOR

MANCHURIA

MOUNTAINS

Selenga River

M   O   N   G   O   L   S

Argan River

• Kobdo

KARA NOR

KERAITS

Orkhon River

Urga ★
(Ulaan Baatar)

KHINGHAN MOUNTAINS

SINKIANG
(CHINESE TURKESTAN)

• Uliastay

TURKS

MOUNTAINS

• Karakoram
(Mongol Court
1234-1256)

HSIUNG-NU or HUNS

TARTARS

45°   M   O   N   G   O   L   I   A   45°

Tsetsenwang

• Tuerin

• Urumchi

Sain Noin Khan •

TSAGAN NOR

Ongin Gol

┌──────────────┐
│ ANDREWS   │
│ 1922, 1923, 1925 │
└──────────────┘

MONGOLIA

ULAN NOR

T   I   E   N

Shabarakh Usu
(Flaming Cliffs)

Iren Dabasu
(Ehrlien)

UIGHURS

S   H   A   N

DUNE DWELLERS

G   O   B   I

Nom Khong •

CHAHAR

• Shangtu
(Xanadu)

TAKLA MAKAN

LOP NOR

D   E   S   E   R   T

┌──────────────┐
│ ANDREWS   │
│ 1928, 1930   │
└──────────────┘

40°   *Tarim River*   G   O   B   I   Urtyn Obo   Kalgan •   **GREAT**   **WALL**   40°

Edsin River

INNER

ONGUT

**Lattimore's
Lost City**

• Kweihwating

★ Peking
(Mongol Court
1256-1368)

• Tientsin

ALA SHAN

Hwang Ho

Gulf of Po Hai

T   I   B   E   T

KANSU

C   H   I   N   A

TANGUT

GREAT WALL

GREAT WALL

NAN SHAN

NINGSIA

• T'ai-Yuan

0   KILOMETERS   200

KOKO NOR

SHENSI

0   MILES   200

90°   100°   110°

This vast sealike desert.

—William of Rubruck, papal envoy to the Mongol court, 1254

In the center of Asia between China and Russia lies the Gobi. In 1919, an American zoologist named Roy Chapman Andrews drove across this desert while shooting mammal specimens for the American Museum of Natural History. He was surprised to see rock formations that he thought were likely to hold fossils, because fossil bones had never been reported from there.

Three years later Andrews went back to the Gobi and discovered some of the richest fossil beds in the world. Five times between 1922 and 1930 he led expeditions to the beds. While the political turmoil in Russia and China spilled into the Gobi, the scientists with Andrews patiently dug the fragments which have formed much of our notion of the past life of the planet.

From the grasslands along the margins of the Gobi came the mounted armies that so often overran the civilizations of Asia and Europe. One of these hordes, and the most successful that the world has ever seen, was led by a tribe of shepherds who called themselves "Mongols." Until the coming of motor vehicles, the nomadic Mongols were too elusive to be controlled by the neighboring settled populace upon whom they sometimes preyed. The first time that many Mongols saw the machines that would change their lives was when Andrews' expeditions drove through their country.

▶▶ *'Obo at Nom Khong or the Sacred Mesa.' Inner Mongolia; summer 1928. J. B. Shackelford, photographer. Two members of the expedition flank the obo. "The Mongols have a custom of building stone-piles called obos, each stone of which is said to represent a prayer to Buddha," wrote two of the expedition's geologists. "All important hilltops are crowned by obos, which enable the grateful topographer to locate points with a precision which in Christian countries would be impossible." Near this obo, the expedition came upon another built entirely of fossils. Photograph courtesy of The American Museum of Natural History.*

To conclude briefly about this country: it is more wretched than I could possible say.

—John of Plano Carpini, papal envoy to the Mongol court, 1247

Desolate it is, but undeniably beautiful.

—Roy Chapman Andrews, 1922

The coasts of the land mass of Europe and Asia are almost everywhere green and fertile. Inland, however, the ground gradually becomes drier, until towards the center it will not support agriculture, and the streams evaporate before they can reach the sea. There stretch the steppes and wastes of Central Asia. In their midst rise the highest mountains in the world, and to the east of these ranges lies the Gobi.

Andrews and his men worked in the Gobi only during the summer, when the prevailing winds brought warm air up from China. On July 1, 1928, they recorded a temperature of 140 degrees Fahrenheit in the sun, but "by ten o'clock in the evening," Andrews noted, "the temperature would drop to 70 degrees, no matter how fiercely the sun had blazed during the day." During the winter, when the prevailing winds blow down from Siberia, temperatures in the Gobi reach 50 degrees below zero.

It took Andrews no more than six days to cross the Gobi in a car. In the days of caravans, Marco Polo reported that "where its breadth is least, it takes a month to cross it, and not a thing to eat is to be found on it. The journey is invariably over either sandy plains or barren mountains; but at the end of each day's march, you stop at a place where water is procurable; not indeed in sufficient quantity for large numbers, but enough to supply fifty or an hundred persons, together with their beasts of burthen." In the crossing, asserted a fifth-century Chinese traveler, one sees "neither birds above, nor beasts below. No guidance is to be obtained save from the rotting bones of dead men which point the way."

▸▸▸ *Cars and members of the Andrews expedition, Inner Mongolia, 1928. Photographer unknown. "We found that the Gobi is essentially a 'rock desert,' with sand-dune belts only in restricted areas," Andrews wrote. "Wind had swept away the lighter material. Day after day we traveled over the nearly barren surface of rock." Photograph courtesy of The American Museum of Natural History.*

The fossils are there, I know they are. Go and find them.

—Henry Fairfield Osborn, president of the American Museum
of Natural History, to Andrews, 1921

"They might as well look for fossils in the Pacific Ocean, as in the Gobi," said his critics when Andrews suggested sending an expedition there. Andrews had to admit that "none of the other geologists who had crossed Mongolia had discovered bones." But, he contended, "what had been done in the past afforded no criterion as to what [the Gobi] might yield to our scientists."

For one thing, Andrews knew from his first trip across the Gobi that cars could be used there. Previous explorers had all gone by camel, averaging only a score of miles a day. With cars, Andrews figured that he could cover hundreds of miles daily, and explore "as much in one season as others have done in ten years." For another thing, Andrews had colleagues at the Museum who had dug fossils in Western America. These paleontologists knew that the American fossils were exposed in great badland basins by the erosion of rain and rivers in an arid climate. "A similar climate prevails over a large part of Central Asia," one of them explained. "If we could locate badlands, we believed that expert collectors could find the extinct animals of Asia as they have found the extinct American animals."

Andrews spent a year appealing to every source he could think of, and finally found backing for an expedition to the Gobi. Its express purpose was to collect specimens of living plants and animals. But Andrews brought along a paleontologist, "partly as a gamble, and partly because the man chosen, Walter Granger, could be counted on to pull more than his own weight whether he had any fossils to collect or not."

The expedition drove into the Gobi on April 21, 1922. Four days later, Andrews wrote, "we heard from the Mongols of a region where bones were to be found; bones 'as big as a man's body,' they said." The expedition headed towards the spot. Just before they reached it, the car carrying Granger stopped off at an outcropping of sedimentary rock. Andrews and the rest went ahead to pitch the tents. "We were hardly settled before Granger's car roared into camp," Andrews wrote in his journal. "The men were obviously excited when I went out to meet them. No one said a word. Granger's eyes were shining and he was puffing violently at his pipe. Silently he dug into his pockets and produced a handful of bone fragments; out of his shirt came a rhinoceros tooth, and the various folds of his upper garments yielded other fossils. He held out his hand: 'Well, Roy, we've done it. The stuff is here.' "

▶▶▶ *'Towing Fulton truck across sand stream.' Inner Mongolia; 1928. J. B. Shackelford, photographer. Andrews' dog rides aloft. "No part of the Gobi," noted two of the expedition's geologists, "is comparable to the extreme dryness of the Atacama desert of Chile, or the Hamada of Egypt." From a few to ten inches of rain fall annually in the Gobi, mostly in the summer. Once after a summer storm had passed, Andrews related, "in its wake lay a narrow trail of white hailstones. Throughout the summer this narrow track over which the hailstones were spread remained as a well-defined band of green. Thus quickly does the desert respond to the slightest moisture." Photograph courtesy of The American Museum of Natural History.*

There were giants in the earth in those days.

—Genesis 6.4

Every season in the field, the expedition found something new. There were the fossil dinosaur eggs, the first ever found anywhere. There were the remains of a Stone Age culture. There were the bones of *Andrewsarchus*, the largest known carnivorous land mammal, and the skull of *Baluchitherium*, the largest mammal that ever walked the earth. The place where they found the dinosaur eggs proved to be one of the richest fossil fields in the world, also yielding skeletons of several new kinds of dinosaurs, traces of early humans, and an inch-long skull in a nodule of sandstone that Granger labeled "an unidentified reptile." It turned out to be one of the oldest known mammals. Of the tens of thousands of specimens they brought back, that skull was "the most precious of all," Andrews felt, because it helped to show when the mammal line had split from the reptiles.

The fossils gave clues to conditions in the past. Bones of the *Baluchitherium* showed that it was eighteen feet tall and proportioned like a horse. Its great height, which fitted it for feeding on trees, its flat teeth, which were suitable for grinding twigs and leaves, and its small hoofs and long legs, which were adapted for running on hard ground, suggest that when it lived the Gobi was lightly forested.

When they dug out a fossil, "if the bone was soft and crumbly, it was hardened with a solution of gum arabic, and Japanese rice paper was stippled on every inch. After this, the specimen was bandaged with strips of burlap soaked in flour paste. When the paste had dried, more of the earth or rock was dug away, and the operations repeated until the entire bone had been enclosed in a hard shell. This kept it intact during the long journey to the Museum."

Once in the central Gobi, Andrews recounted, "while working on the face of an escarpment near the camp, the men were annoyed by the brown pit viper, *Agkistrodon halys intermedius*, which was present there in numbers. When the sun began to warm the rocks near noon, these extremely poisonous reptiles would crawl out from their nests among the rocks and prevent the fossil collectors from becoming drowsy over their work. Each man usually accounted for five or ten during the day."

➤➤➤ '*R. C. Andrews collecting young kites.' Urtyn Obo, Inner Mongolia; July 1926. J. B. Shackelford, photographer. It was in badlands such as these that the Gobi fossils were usually found. Once, wrote Andrews, "I discovered an eagle's nest—a great pile of sticks and branches which must have been carried a long distance, since we had seen no wood for miles. Near the nest were the remains of at least twenty antelopes." Photograph courtesy of The American Museum of Natural History.*

Once, Andrews related, "it was the hour just before daylight when consciousness is drowned in heaviest sleep. Suddenly I sat up, wide awake, with a strange feeling of unrest. Slipping out of my fur bag I stepped through the tent door. There was a stillness in the air, vaguely depressing. It made me shiver and I buckled on a cartridge belt and revolver before circling the tents. All was quiet. Even the camels, kneeling in two long double lines, nose to nose, were sleeping. It was the tomblike stillness that made it so disturbing. Fifteen minutes passed when I slowly became conscious that the air was vibrating to a continuous even roar which was getting louder every second. Suddenly I understood it all. One of the terrible desert storms was on the way.

"It came like a cyclone bringing a swirling red cloud of dust. In less than ten minutes the temperature dropped at least thirty degrees. A thousand shrieking demons seemed to be pelting my face with sand and gravel." Trying to walk "was like pushing into a yellow wall. We could not see twenty feet, but we heard the clatter of tins, the sharp rip of canvas, and then a tumbling mass of camp beds, tables, chairs, bags, and pails swept down the hill. Lying flat on the ground with our faces buried in wet clothes we at least could breathe.

"The gale continued for an hour and then dropped suddenly into a flat calm. Not a breath of wind stirred the flag which hung limply above my tent, whipped almost to ribbons. We began to dig out the tents and empty the sand from our clothes and beds. Much of the Gobi was in our belongings; it had sifted into even the tightest boxes. The cameras, rifles, pistols and field-glasses suffered most, for even their double cases could not keep them clean. The windshield glass of the cars was so badly sand-blasted that eventually it had to be removed."

▸▸▸ *'Expedition campment.' Tsetsenwang, Outer Mongolia; June 1922. R. C. Andrews, photographer. In addition to cars and trucks, the expeditions led by Andrews employed camels. Their loads are in the foreground. On the outward journey, they carried mostly fuel for the cars; leakage was 50 percent the first season. On the return, they hauled fossils. The tents, of Mongol design, were better able to withstand the Gobi windstorms than tents with "walls." Andrews' tent, to the left of the center, was dark blue and marked with yellow bats, symbols of fortune in Mongolia. Photograph courtesy of The American Museum of Natural History.*

Chinggis Khan used to say that the hunting of wild beasts was the proper occupation for the commanders of armies.

—Juvaini, ca. 1255

"Please, Master, tomorrow must catch antelope; just now no have got many meat." With this the Chinese cook would notify the Andrews expedition that it was time for a hunt. "On the morrow," wrote Granger, "two men, one to drive and one to shoot, start out in the touring car to hunt the game of the country, which consists principally of two species of gazelles.

"The gazelles are wary creatures but they have a fatal habit of crossing in front of any fast-moving object which is traveling in their general direction. The experienced hunter does not chase the gazelles with the car but drives slowly along parallel with the herd until it is about to cross over, then he puts on full speed, swings slightly away from the herd and tries to force it to cross within 200 yards. At the point of crossing the driver puts on all brakes, and the hunter, who is already out on the running board, steps off and usually gets in three or four shots before the yellow streaks are out of range."

The Mongol emperors used to hunt the same kinds of animals by commanding tens of thousands of troops to surround a plain and drive the game inward. For weeks or even months the troops moved towards the center, watching day and night that no beasts broke through their lines. "Finally," related a Persian witness, "when the ring has been contracted to a diameter of [about ten miles], they bind ropes together and cast felts over them; while the troops come to a halt all around the ring, standing shoulder to shoulder. The ring is now filled with the cries and commotion of every kind of game, tigers becoming familiar with wild asses, wolves intimate with hares. When the ring has been so much contracted that the wild beasts are unable to stir, first the Khan rides in and slays some with a bow and arrows, then, after he has wearied of the sport, he dismounts upon high ground to watch the princes likewise entering the ring. Several days pass in this manner."

Once, according to legend, "the Khan had seated himself upon a hilltop in order to view the scene, whereupon the beasts of every kind set their faces towards his throne and set up a wailing and lamentation like that of petitioners for justice. The Khan commanded that they should be set free."

►►► *'Bighorn ram and two Mongols.' Shensi, North China; 1921. R. C. Andrews, photographer. The sheep pictured here belongs to a North Chinese race,* Ovis ammon comosa, *the males of which can weigh 225 pounds. The Gobi or Altai bighorn,* Ovis ammon ammon, *is twice as large. Marco Polo reported that the horns of wild sheep were used to make stirrup irons and horseshoes. Photograph courtesy of The American Museum of Natural History.*

The sand defeated us.

—Andrews, after twice trying to explore the western Gobi

"I understand now how thirst can make a man half insane," wrote the Swedish explorer Sven Hedin in April 1895. His party had run out of water while trying to cross part of the Takla Makan, a westward extension of the Gobi filled with sand dunes and laced with beds of streams that flow out onto the sands and dry up. As he watched, three of the men "gathered a saucepanful of the camels' urine. They poured it into an iron cup, added vinegar and sugar, then holding their noses they swallowed the concoction. After a while they were seized with violent and painful vomiting, which completely prostrated them."

Now only Hedin and one other man, Kasim, were fit to travel. They waited until the cool of night, then, leaving the others with the supplies, they struck off towards a dry riverbed where they hoped to find pools of water. Hedin had dressed himself entirely in white. "If I was doomed to die in the sand," he wrote, "I wanted to be properly attired.

"The night was pitch dark. The stars twinkled in the pure atmosphere, but their light was too faint to enable us to judge the ground. We were stopped by every sand dune we came to. We would walk down a slope, then all of a sudden a wall of sand would rise up immediately in front of us." They would climb to the top of the dune, slide down to the other side, then make their way to the next. "I crept long distances on my hands and knees," wrote Hedin. In this manner, without water, they continued for five nights.

Once, they saw a tamarisk tree: "That solitary tree reminded me of a water-lily swimming, as it were, on the billowy surface of the desert ocean." They chewed its leaves for moisture, but "our throats were on fire. We could not talk, only whisper or hiss out our words."

When the sun rose on the sixth day, "the horizon had a different outline from what we were accustomed to see. After going a little farther, we perceived that the horizon was edged with a black border." It was a line of trees growing along a riverbed. Hedin reached the water that evening. Kasim reached it the next morning. One of the men they had left behind reached it with two camels that same day. The other men and beasts never did. The next winter, local hunters following fox tracks over the dunes came upon the camp where the supplies had been abandoned. The tent, still standing, was buried under six feet of sand. The remains of the dead men were not found.

▶▶▶ *'Camels crossing dunes at Tsagan Nor for water.' Outer Mongolia; 1925. J. B. Shackelford, photographer. The Gobi camel is the two-humped Bactrian,* Camelus bactrianus. *In the winter it grows a thick mantle of wool. There are small herds of wild Bactrian camels in Chinese Turkestan, but some say they are descended from domestic stock. No wild dromedaries exist. Photograph courtesy of The American Museum of Natural History.*

The qualities of the shepherd—courage, love of fighting, and contempt of hunger and hardship, rather than the industrious character of the peasant.

—Eduard E. Evans-Pritchard, 1940

When the horse was first domesticated on the Eurasian steppes in about 5000 B.C., it was no larger than a light pony. Surely from the beginning it was casually ridden, but it could not carry men much farther or faster than they could go on their own feet. Its main value to the Bronze Age civilizations of the Old World was as a drawer of plows, carts, and chariots.

The desire for larger draft animals led to the horse being bred up to a size which made it useful as a mount. This happened about 1000 B.C. In the centuries that followed, cavalry replaced chariots everywhere, and the horse became "the foundation of military might, the great resource of the state," as a Chinese general of the first century B.C. put it.

It was easier to raise horses on the virgin grasslands of the steppe than in the farming countries to the south, where giving pastures to horses meant depriving people of land to till. The steppe dwellers, who had been hunters and marginal farmers who kept small flocks, began to raise great herds of horses, which they drove south and sold in China, India, and Persia. It was then, when horse raising became profitable, that the Gobi tribes became nomads, so they would be free to lead their horses to ever greener pastures.

▸▸▸ *'Small boy lama and Mongol father.' Urga, Outer Mongolia; July 1919. Yvette Borup Andrews, photographer. "From early childhood they were taught to ride on sheep, to draw the bow, and shoot birds and rats," wrote a Chinese historian in the first century B.C. Andrews commented that "the Mongols have no respect whatever for someone who cannot ride." The Mongol horseman wears a plum-colored robe. His hat is of fur and black velvet with a yellow crown and streamers of red ribbon or peacock feathers at the back, depending on his rank. Photograph courtesy of The American Museum of Natural History.*

> The people who at present inhabit those deserts know only that their
> ancestors have formerly conquered the world.
>
> —Voltaire

The Gobi has seen the passage of many peoples. Perhaps the first were Stone Age hunters whose remains were found by the Andrews expedition. Such numbers of their campsites are scattered among the dunes that Andrews was led to proclaim, "twenty thousand years ago Mongolia was much more densely populated than it is today." The Dune Dwellers, as they have been named, left millions of chipped stone tools. They also left grinders, which show that they gathered wild grains. But their bones are too rare for us to judge if they were the ancestors of the next people to appear in the Gobi. These were settled farmers who tilled the soils of the oases and riverbanks. Between 6000 and 3000 B.C. they acquired domestic animals. Later they became nomads who in the fourth century B.C. entered history as the Hsiung-nu of the Chinese annals, "wandering about in search of pastures and water." The Hsiung-nu were known to the West as the Huns, and they almost certainly spoke a Turkic language. Until the tenth century A.D. various Turkic peoples held most of the Gobi and the adjoining steppes. They had few permanent abodes, but the valley of the Orkhon River in what is now central Mongolia, where their earliest inscriptions have been found, was their heartland.

In the first centuries A.D., the Gobi Turks subjugated the hunting tribes who lived in the forests north and east of the desert. Legend says these hunters were generated from the union of a fallow deer and a blue wolf, two forest creatures, "who came, passing over the Tenggis," or sea, which is Lake Baikal in the midst of the Siberian forest. As slaves, servants, and soldiers of the Turkic nomads, these hunters entered the Gobi and there learned shepherd ways. Their numbers had grown enough by the eighth century so that they could challenge their masters' claim to parts of the desert range. At the end of the twelfth century one of their chiefs, Chinggis Khan, conquered the entire Gobi and ended there forever the rule of the Turks. As Chinggis' tribe was called "Mongol," this name was afterwards adopted by many of the tribes under his sway, including one known as "Ta-ta" in the Chinese annals and called "Tartars" in the West. Today the word "Mongol" also characterizes the physical type and the group of tongues spoken by the forest tribes who took over the Gobi.

▶▶▶ *'Yurt interior.' Outer Mongolia; June 1922. R. C. Andrews, photographer. The yurt, a sort of heavy tent, is the main type of dwelling in the Gobi. The collapsible latticework frame is covered with felts to form the walls. The brazier in the foreground holds* argol—dung—*the fuel of the Gobi nomads. Photograph courtesy of The American Museum of Natural History.*

> This is his strength: he is the desire of them all.
>
> —Borte, Chinggis Khan's principal wife, upon hearing that he was consorting
> with a Turkish queen

Around 1167 the wife of a Mongol chief bore a son. Tradition says that when the baby entered the world he held in his fist "a clot of blood the size of a knucklebone." He was named Temujin, meaning "iron," after a Turkish chief his father had just captured.

On the eastern steppes at that time, relates the Mongol chronicle, "the many peoples were at strife. Not entering into their beds, they were spoiling one another." When Temujin was ten, his father was poisoned by his enemies. Rivalries within their clan caused his mother to be exiled. She and her seven small children wandered for several years as outcasts, fishing, hunting birds, and digging roots and wild onions for food. Temujin was captured by his father's enemies and forced to go among their camps wearing a wooden collar. One night, near a river, he broke away, "and suffering his collar to flow down along the water, he lay with only his face exposed," and escaped.

He then claimed and married a girl who had been betrothed to him before his father's death. This union gave him a standing within his clan. Over the next twenty years he vied for mastery, first of his own tribe, then of all the steppe tribes. He allied himself with Ong Khan, the Christian chief of a Turkish tribe, and together they subdued most of their neighbors. When a quarrel between the two men led to war, Temujin emerged as ruler of all the tribes of the eastern steppes and, in 1206, took the title of Chinggis (Genghis) Khan, the "oceanic" or universal ruler.

He soon began the conquest of China, which would not end until the time of his grandson Kublai's rule. In 1211 he breached the Great Wall. Peking fell in 1215. After that he reduced the peoples of the western steppes, then the Moslem Khwarizmian Empire, which included parts of Iran, Afghanistan, and southeast Russia. He sent an army south of the Caspian Sea across the Caucasus Mountains into Russia, where it ravaged the Ukraine before rejoining Chinggis' main force near the Aral Sea. In 1226 he again took up the conquest of North China, where he died the next year, either from a knife wound given him by a consort queen or from a fall from his horse. At his secret grave, "forty slave-girls and as many horses were dispatched to join their master in the next world."

Witnesses say he was "of tall stature, vigorous build, with cat's eyes, and a wide forehead." His dominions were divided among his four sons: two received portions each equal in area to all of Europe; the others got lands about one-third as large.

►►► *Urga, Outer Mongolia; May 1922. J. B. Shackelford, photographer. "Yesterday we photoed a Mongol giant whom I had seen in 1918," Andrews entered in his journal. "The man is 7 ft. 4 in. tall and weighed 307 pounds. He had been sent in former years as a present by the Mongol Government to the Czar of Russia. The Czar found him a 'White Elephant' and after decorating him returned him to the Mongols with thanks and compliments." Photograph courtesy of The American Museum of Natural History.*

They destroy kingdoms as one tears up grass. Why does heaven permit it?

—A Tangut, after Chinggis Khan invaded his country

"What shall I write now, concerning the pain and misfortune of this time?" asked a Persian who witnessed the Mongol invasions. One historian relates that a Mongol general promised the people of a Chinese town, " 'Make me a present of ten thousand swallows and a thousand cats, and I will cease attacking.' The swallows and cats were sent. Lighted wool was fastened to their tails and they were let loose. They returned to their nests and their homes, and setting the town afire, enabled the Mongols to enter "— without attacking, as the general had promised. When the Mongols took Peking the looting continued for a month. Girls threw themselves from the walls to avoid falling into their hands, "the soil was greasy with human fat," and "a vast heap of human bones" lay by the main gate. The governor of Peking committed suicide; his daughter was carried off to the steppes. The emperor of North China climbed onto his own funeral pyre. A boy emperor of South China fled in a boat and was drowned.

In what is now northeast Iran and Moslem Russia, the inhabitants of half the cities were massacred. "Rose gardens became furnaces," recorded a chronicler. When a Mongol prince was killed at the siege of a town, "in the exaction of vengeance not even dogs and cats were left alive." At another, finding no stones that could be used in their catapults, the Mongols cut down whole groves of mulberry trees (on which the silkworm is raised) and used the trunks instead. Still unable to capture the town, they diverted the Oxus River and washed it away. For the next three centuries the river ran into the Caspian Sea instead of the Aral. The Mongols dammed the Tigris, took Baghdad, shut the Abbassid caliph in a tower with his jewels and allowed him to starve.

The Mongols attacked European Russia in the winter after sending a sorceress "demanding one tenth of everything: of men and princes and horses—of everything one tenth." Kiev was burned, and its prince suffocated under planks that the Mongols sat upon and dined. In Central Europe, they collected nine sacks of right ears from their fallen enemies in one battle, displayed the duke of Silesia's head on a pole, chased the king of Hungary to a castle on the Adriatic, and pitched his linen tent on their Asian pastures.

"How dost thou know whom God forgives?" the Great Khan of the Mongols wrote to the Pope. "You of the west believe that you alone are men of God and despise all others. But we have conquered the whole earth from the east to the west, and if this were not by the power of God, what could men have done?"

▸▸▸ *Entrance to the Urga Prison, Urga, Outer Mongolia; May 1922. R. C. Andrews, photographer. The sign above the door reads "Residence of the Jailor [lit., protecting chief] and soldiers." When Andrews first visited the prison in 1919, he saw "small rooms, almost dark. In these dungeons were piled wooden boxes, four feet by two and one-half feet high. These coffins are the prisoners' cells. Some of the poor wretches have heavy chains about their necks and both hands manacled together. They can neither sit erect nor lie at full length." When he visited the prison again in 1922, the practice had been abolished and the prisoners "all seemed to be well fed and clothed." Photograph courtesy of The American Museum of Natural History.*

That same year foreigners came in countless numbers, like locusts.
God alone knows who they are and whence they came out.

—Russian chronicle, referring to the Mongols, 1223

The Mongol trooper carried a cooking kettle, a set of tools, and felts which, combined with those of others, would make a tent. He had up to a score of horses, depending on the length of the campaign. From the mares he took milk, and on this and some dried milk curd that he carried, he could live for months. His main weapon was the bow. It was made of wood, horn, and sinew, was double curved, and had a heavier draw and a longer range than an English longbow. He usually carried two bows and several quivers of arrows, some light "with small sharp points for long-range shooting and pursuit," others heavy "with large broad heads for close quarters." The arrowheads cut two ways, could pierce armor, and were sometimes poisoned. His armor was slabs of boiled hide. In winter he wore furs.

Soldiers were grouped in ranks by tens. Nine men obeyed a tenth, nine commanders of ten obeyed another, and so on. By contrast with the armies of the Christians, Moslems, or Chinese, one observer noted that in the Mongol army "there is a true equality. No difference is made between them, no attention being paid to wealth and power." Adolescents were often in the ranks; captives and mercenaries were put in the van. The numbers of Mongol soldiers were usually fewer than those of their adversaries; when they invaded North China in 1211 with 110,000 men, their enemy had four times as many. In 1221, the Mongols took 150,000 men on their expedition to the west, and defeated a force three times as large.

The Mongols fought on horseback. "They never mix with the enemy," said Marco Polo, "but keep hovering about him, discharging their arrows first from one side and then from the other, occasionally pretending to fly, and during their flight, shooting arrows backwards at their pursuers, killing men and horses, as if they were combating face to face." Witnesses stressed "the speed, silence, and mechanical perfection" of the movements of their squadrons.

"What army in the whole world can equal the Mongol army?" asked a Persian minister. Even today their mobility would be a wonder. Chinggis Khan once led his soldiers 130 miles in two days over some of the highest and roughest country in Afghanistan. One of his grandsons took an army 180 miles over the Carpathian Mountains in three days. "It is for you to fly and for us to pursue," another grandson told the Mamelukes after the Mongols took Damascus. "And whither will you fly, and by what road shall you escape us?"

▶▶▶ *'Feast after meet.' Tsagen Nor, Outer Mongolia; July 1922. R. C. Andrews, photographer. Behind the men and boys is a yurt. The boxes of stones on the roof hold down the felts with which it is covered. Photograph courtesy of The American Museum of Natural History.*

A host whose onslaught was like a hurricane, a people
who had never known a city.

—One of the earliest known references to steppe nomads,
inscription at Ur, ca. 1950 B.C.

Even after the Mongols had made themselves rulers of much of the civilized world, they had not built one permanent city in all of the steppes. Of their capital in Mongolia, a Dutch friar sent there by the pope in 1253 wrote, "You must know that exclusive of the palace of the Khan, it is not as big as the village of Saint Denis, and the monastery of Saint Denis is ten times larger than the palace." Riding west from the capital, he wrote, "in two months and ten days we never saw a town, nor the trace of any building save tombs, with the exception of one little village," until he reached the Volga, over two thousand miles away. He passed through one place where "there used to be many towns, but most of them were destroyed, so that the [Mongols] might graze there."

Historians relate that in 1226, after the Mongols had subdued much of northern China, "it was seriously proposed, not in the hour of victory and passion, but in calm deliberate council, to exterminate all the inhabitants of that populous country, that the vacant land might be converted to the pasture of cattle," as Edward Gibbon put it. Those favoring the proposition said that the people yielded no revenue, as they had either hidden themselves or sought refuge in the temples.

But one of Chinggis' ministers argued, "How can it be said that the people are useless? When your majesty will conquer the south your armies will need supplies. If we establish a fair administration throughout the country, we can annually obtain 500,000 ounces of silver, 80,000 bolts of silk, and more than 400,000 bushels of grain." With this Chinggis ordered that the carnage of the campaign should lessen and the population be spared. And afterwards, wrote Jorge Luis Borges, "the Mongol horsemen who wanted to turn China into an infinite pasture grew old in the cities they had longed to destroy."

▸▸▸ *Sain Noin Khan Lamasery, 300 miles southwest of Urga, Outer Mongolia; June or July 1922. Walter Granger, photographer; one of a three-piece panorama. At the beginning of the twentieth century there were practically no permanent buildings in Mongolia except lamaseries, and it is estimated that half the people in Mongolia were under direct religious jurisdiction, either as serfs "owned" by the temples or as lamas. Andrews thought that two-thirds of the males were lamas. They lived in "cities" like the one partially shown here. They were forbidden to marry or hold property. They produced nothing. Prior to 1922, when the present government began to suppress Lamaism, the population of Mongolia had been decreasing. Photograph courtesy of The American Museum of Natural History.*

> After us the descendants of our clan will wear gold-embroidered garments,
> eat rich and sweet food, ride fine horses, and embrace beautiful women, but
> they will forget us and these great times.
>
> —Chinggis Khan, ca. 1206

Chinggis Khan's grandson Kublai was the sovereign of the largest empire that was ever controlled by one man. His rule in China was absolute. His brother and cousins ruled in Persia, Russia, and Central Asia, but they all acknowledged his authority.

When Kublai became emperor of the Mongols in 1260, he moved the capital from the steppes north of the Gobi down to Peking. There he built Taitu, his great court, at the center of which was a palace "covered with gold and silver—so vast, so rich, and so beautiful," wrote Marco Polo, "that no man on earth could design anything superior to it." A hundred miles north of his great court Kublai built Shangtu, or Xanadu, his upper court. There a wall enclosed "rich and beautiful meadows, watered by many rivulets, where a variety of animals of the deer and goat kind are pastured." When Kublai hunted at Xanadu, wrote Polo, "he has small leopards carried on horseback, behind their keepers, and when he pleases [they jump to the ground] and instantly seize a stag, goat, or fallow deer." He traveled in a chamber borne on the backs of four elephants. His bodyguard was a corps of Christian soldiers from the northern shores of the Black Sea. A lion was trained to approach his throne and do him obeisance.

Once when Kublai displayed as captive a boy emperor of South China, his wife was troubled and remarked, "There has been no imperial family which lasted 1,000 years, and who dare say I and my children may not suffer the fate of this boy?" Less than a century later, the Mongols were expelled from China amidst flood, famine, and rebellion. The last Mongol emperor fled back to the steppes and died in a tent, lamenting the loss of his "great fortress of Taitu, where I sat holding the name and sway of my peoples."

The ramparts of Taitu have long since made way for the walls of succeeding dynasties. As for Xanadu, a French priest who visited the spot in 1845 found, in place of the palaces and parks, "a large, busy, bustling dirty town, with a great manufactory of images of Buddha."

►►► *'Tartar wall.' Peking, China. Date and photographer unknown. "Tartar" here refers to the Manchus, a Manchurian tribe who ruled China from the seventeenth to the twentieth century. Their brick walls are larger than the pounded dirt walls that the Mongols built around Peking, which were about 30 feet high and 17 miles long. Photograph courtesy of The American Museum of Natural History.*

Formerly there were several cities. Now all but two are buried in sand.

—Ninth-century Persian geography, referring to the Takla Makan

"It was while travelling [in the Gobi] with one Mongol companion, with no particular destination in mind, that I began to hear stories of a ruined city," wrote the explorer Owen Lattimore in 1932. "I asked to see the city, and my Mongol companion took me there without any difficulty. The country has been traversed repeatedly by recent travellers and it is pure accident that the city has not previously been noticed."

Walls a quarter of a mile on each side and twelve feet high in places surrounded "ruins of buildings of remarkable size for so small a city. Great heaps of brick and stone and the outlines of solidly built foundations proved that there had once been public buildings of real grandeur far out here in the steppe. The most remarkable thing in the city, however, which immediately drew my attention, was a collection of seven stone slabs marked with crosses of the kind known as 'Nestorian.' "

Nestorianism was a heretical Christian sect that was centered in Syria in the fifth century. The advance of Islam pushed it across Central Asia, where several of the nomad tribes adopted it. Chinggis Khan's last rival on the steppes was a Nestorian. Kublai Khan's mother and favorite wife were Nestorians. A papal envoy reported in 1253 that Nestorian priests followed the Mongol court "as flies do honey."

A group of scholars who visited the site a few years after Lattimore found inscriptions that said a prince named K'uo-li-ki-syu had ruled over the city. The Chinese dynastic annals state that K'uo-li-ki-syu was a Nestorian prince who had in fact reigned in the region of the city that Lattimore found. His mother was a daughter of Kublai Khan, and he himself married successively one of Kublai's granddaughters and one of his great-granddaughters. Lattimore heard a legend from the local people that the city was ruined because "its lord married a daughter of the Mongol emperor and then plotted to seize the throne. His wife betrayed him to her father, 'who sent troops that destroyed everything.' "

▸▸▸ *'Prayer shrine,' and lama. Sain Noin Khan Lamasery, 300 miles southwest of Urga, Outer Mongolia; June 1922. R. C. Andrews, photographer. Lamaism is a form of Tibetan Buddhism with elements of shamanism, the old religion of the Mongols. Lamaism replaced shamanism in Mongolia in the thirteenth century following Kublai's adoption of Tibetan Buddhism. Photograph courtesy of The American Museum of Natural History.*

On July 13, 1923, George Olsen, a geologist with Andrews, reported that he had found some fossil eggs. "We did not take his story very seriously," Andrews recalled, because they were digging in deposits of dinosaur remains, and no one had ever discovered dinosaur eggs before. "We felt quite certain that his so-called eggs would prove to be sandstone concretions or some other geological phenomena." Nevertheless, they all went to have a look.

"In a small sandstone ledge were lying three eggs partly broken," Andrews continued. "The brown shell was so egg-like that there could be no mistake. Granger finally said, 'No dinosaur eggs have ever been found, but the reptiles probably did lay eggs. These must be dinosaur eggs. They can't be anything else.'

"The prospect was thrilling, but we would not let ourselves think of it too seriously, and continued to criticize the supposition from every possible standpoint. Finally we had to admit that we could make them out to be nothing else."

The members of the expedition gathered all the loose bits of eggshell. A large part of the sandstone ledge was removed and sent to the American Museum. Subsequently, the block was found to contain thirteen eggs in two layers lying exactly as they had been left by the dinosaur when she covered them with sand 95 million years before. An-

drews guessed that after the dinosaur laid the eggs, she had covered them with a thin layer of sand and left them to be hatched by the sun. A windstorm blew more sand over them. "Air and the sun's warmth were cut off, and incubation ceased. The weight of the heaped-up sand eventually cracked the shells, the liquid contents ran out, and extremely fine sand sifted into the interiors, preventing the eggs from being entirely crushed, and later forming cores of red sandstone." In two fossil eggs there even remained the delicate skeletons of embryo dinosaurs.

The following season, near where the eggs had been found, the expedition came across signs of Stone Age humans. In one place, there were bits of dinosaur eggshell that had been worked into squares. "Then we realized," Andrews noted, "that these people were the original discoverers of the dinosaur eggs."

▸▸▸ *'Granger at work on the nest of dinosaur eggs found by Lovell.' Shabarakh Usu (the Flaming Cliffs), 300 miles south of Urga, Outer Mongolia; 1925. J. B. Shackelford, photographer. "It was a delicate operation to remove [the eggs]," wrote Andrews. "When the wind blew, Granger had to lie full length to avoid being swept over the brink." A yurt is pitched on the plain beyond the cliffs. Photograph courtesy of The American Museum of Natural History.*

How little we are able to judge from the ordinary habits of life, on what circumstances, occurring only at long intervals, the rarity or extinction of a species may be determined.

—Charles Darwin, 1833

At the same geologic moment on land and in the sea the bones of dinosaurs cease to appear in the rocks, while the remains of other kinds of life go on accumulating without a halt. Their extinction has been ascribed to a sudden chilling of the earth that killed them off while sparing warm-blooded and lower forms upon which the cold had less effect. But it is unlikely that cold alone could have exterminated them either in the seas, where extremes of temperature are mitigated, or on the land, where even plants susceptible to the cold continued to flourish as before. One might imagine some fatal disease wiping them out without leaving a trace of itself. But it is hard to see how a disease could have destroyed such a broad range of reptiles as the dinosaurs without killing off the rest of the reptiles as well.

The Andrews expeditions found proof that dinosaurs, like most modern reptiles, laid eggs. Whether or not dinosaurs tended their nests and protected their young, we will never know. Few modern reptiles do. When the dinosaurs left this earth, its inheritors were tiny mammals like the fossil ones dug up by the Andrews expeditions. Mammals can maintain their body heat independently of their surroundings. Reptiles cannot; when the temperature falls, reptiles get sluggish. Among dinosaurs, cold spells must have been times of truce, when predator and prey drowsed together. It might be that the early mammals broke this truce and came in the cold to eat the eggs or small offspring of the dinosaurs. In this way, the dinosaur line would have become extinct even while the adults went unchallenged.

Perhaps the living reptiles survived because they developed defenses that the dinosaurs did not have. The turtles, which secrete their eggs in pits, have carried their shells with them since the beginning of the age of dinosaurs. Crocodiles, alligators, and snakes, many of which guard their eggs in lairs, are so stealthy that even man has trouble catching them. Lizards are too small or too quick to be more than occasional prey for lucky birds or mammals. And one iguana-like reptile, little changed since the time of the dinosaurs, survives on Pacific islands where no mammals have ever lived.

▸▸▸ *'House of the brother of the Living God.' Urga, Outer Mongolia; July 5, 1919. Yvette Borup Andrews, photographer. The Living God, or "Hutuktu," was the third most holy of the living incarnations of Buddha. The last one died in 1923, and the present government has not allowed a successor to be picked. Andrews noted that in accordance with their religious beliefs, the Mongols did not bury their dead but threw them out to be devoured by the wolves, dogs, and birds. Near where this picture was taken, he wrote, "I obtained a fine series of skulls for anthropomorphic study." Photograph courtesy of The American Museum of Natural History.*

That unknown world, immeasurably far removed, where man was not.

—W. H. Hudson

In 1928, on his way back to camp, Granger stepped on a fragment of bone which proved to be the lower jaw of a new type of mastodon. "The spatulate front of the jaw can be described only as resembling a great coal shovel. Side by side in the end were two flat teeth. They were eighteen inches across. The jaw itself was more than five feet long," and he guessed it had served for "scooping up succulent water plants."

Two years later, the expedition discovered "an amphitheater in some badlands. The slopes were strewn thickly with broken mastodon bones—teeth, skulls, vertebrae, ribs. Clearly," wrote Andrews, "it was the site of a former bog. When we removed the upper cover of sand, a mass of fossil bones was disclosed in a thick lens of green clay. Great scoop-jaws were heaped upon each other in every possible position. Mixed with them in a seemingly hopeless jumble were enormous flat shoulder-blades, pelvic bones, limbs, and scores of ribs.

"It was difficult to remove any bone, for usually it lay under several others. Only by finding the topmost ones could the two paleontologists and their five assistants begin the excavating. The bones themselves were like chalk." Andrews was eager to help, but "after I dug into a jaw, Granger politely suggested that I cease. I retired to the outskirts where I could watch and drift back to the days when it all happened."

The climate was different then. A lake covered the land. Andrews surmised that "lush vegetation lined the shores. Floating plants sent their roots downward through the shallow water into a well of mud. A huge mastodon, his monstrous shovel-jaw dredging up masses of trailing grasses, worked his way slowly along the shore. The succulent vegetation resting innocently just beyond the water's edge enticed him farther and farther into the treacherous mud. Suddenly, amidst his feeding he found that he could not lift his leg. He struggled madly only to sink deeper into the mire of death.

"Another came and still others, each one to die as he had died. Down in the black mud tons of flesh dropped away from the great skeletons, leaving the bones to separate one by one. Perhaps at last the death-trap was full to overflowing; perhaps the water, fouled by decaying flesh, sickened the vegetable life and left the trap unbaited." Eventually the great lake dried up, and over thousands of centuries what had been mud became rock.

One of the mastodons was an adult female. "In the pelvic cavity were the skull and jaws of an unborn baby."

▶▶▶ 'Our caravan.' Outer Mongolia, 45 miles northeast of Urga; July 1919. Yvette Borup Andrews, photographer. North of the Gobi the land grades from desert to prairie to forest. Open stands of larch like the one in the background are the first trees to appear on the better-watered north slopes. Often these stands are composed of sets of trees of uniform size because they all were germinated during periods of comparatively high rainfall coming between dryer periods when no seedlings sprouted. Like most deserts, the Gobi is getting larger. The American explorer Owen Lattimore reported that he saw places on the Gobi's margins where the Mongols had chained down the last surviving remnants of the forests of wetter times. Photograph courtesy of The American Museum of Natural History.

I am without money—will you not lend me your purse?

—Common form of address of Gobi brigands

"Brigands must be considered in every expedition to the interior of Mongolia," Andrews wrote. "Usually they are soldier-deserters from unpaid or defeated armies." In 1922, the caravan that carried fuel for the expedition's cars was "attacked by small parties of brigands five or six times, but the robbers had been driven off by rifle fire from several of our men and a Mongol soldier who was attached to the caravan."

In 1928, he reported, "our caravan met five thousand camels just down from Urga [the Mongolian capital]. Accompanying them was a bandit 'liaison officer.' A few years before he had been a respectable landlord of one of the motor inns on the Urga trail. I knew him well and knew that now he was a head brigand. What is more, he knew that I knew it. He posed as a 'general' who could arrange protection for our caravan through his 'soldiers.' Half an hour of tea-drinking and extraneous conversation ensued before we got around to business. He suggested the customary fee of five dollars a camel. I offered one dollar. He knew that our boxes contained nothing that his brigands could use or sell, and eventually we settled on half the usual amount."

Brigands proved less dangerous than politicians. In Urga, Andrews related, "the officials seemed to feel that it was not reasonable that an expedition with so many camels and motor cars, and obviously costing such a large sum of money, could be coming to Mongolia merely for scientific work. We were under constant surveillance."

In 1925, Andrews was twice called out of the field to deal with officials in Urga. Thereafter, he decided to explore only in the Chinese part of the Gobi. In 1926 and 1927, civil war in North China kept the expedition from leaving Peking. In 1928, Andrews had to pay large sums to both the brigands and the Chinese officials before he could go into the field. The following year, the new Chinese government would not let him take any more fossils out of their country. Finally in 1931, with the worldwide depression compounding his diplomatic problems, he had to quit.

Andrews never returned to the Gobi. He stayed in New York, became director of the American Museum in 1934, and died in 1960 at the age of seventy-six.

▸▸▸ *'Cars and cavalry escort outside Kalgan.' North China, near the Great Wall; 1928. J. Makenzie Young, photographer. "When we were about to start in the morning," Andrews related, "their commander sent an officer to say that for our safety he had dispatched men beyond us on the road. He ended by remarking, 'Please don't shoot my soldiers!'" Towers like those behind the road were set in a line from the Great Wall to Peking. "At the approach of the invader," explained the Russian explorer Prejevalsky, a fire was lighted in each tower and "the news was conveyed with marvellous rapidity." Photograph courtesy of The American Museum of Natural History.*

More than six months were employed
in the tranquil journey of a caravan from Samarcand to Pekin.

—Edward Gibbon, 1788

Caravans carrying silk must have spanned the deserts of Central Asia long before the first century A.D., when a Greek wrote of the Chinese, "who are famous for the woolen substance obtained from their forests which enables the Roman matron to flaunt transparent raiment in public."

Cities grew up along the caravan routes, and prospered or suffered according to the fortunes of trade. The rise of ocean-going commerce between East and West caused most of them to be abandoned by the nineteenth century, when a traveler in the Gobi wrote of seeing "a great forsaken city, with battlemented ramparts, watchtowers, and four great gates, all sunk into the earth and covered with a thick turf."

Andrews arrived in the Gobi at the same time as the car. When he first drove across the desert he wrote, "I wish I could make those who spend their lives within a city know how strange and out of place that motor seemed, alone there upon the open plain on the borders of Mongolia. I felt half ashamed to admit to myself as the miles sped by

that the springy seat was more comfortable than the saddle on my Mongol pony. I realized then that, for better or for worse, the sanctity of the desert was gone forever. The secrets which were yielded up to but a chosen few are open now to all, and the world will speed across the miles of rolling prairie, hearing nothing, feeling nothing, knowing nothing. Camels will still plod their silent way across the age-old plains, but the mystery is lost."

▸▸▸ *'Looking down from atop Flaming Cliffs at caravan.' Shabarakh Usu, near the Flaming Cliffs, Outer Mongolia; July 1925. J. B. Shackelford, photographer. "Certain old men can 'recognize' the smell of the earth of a road or region when traveling at night," claimed Owen Lattimore. "Such an old man will dismount, take up a handful of earth, sniff at it and say: 'No, this is not our road; we should go in that other direction.'" Photograph courtesy of The American Museum of Natural History.*

SIBERIA

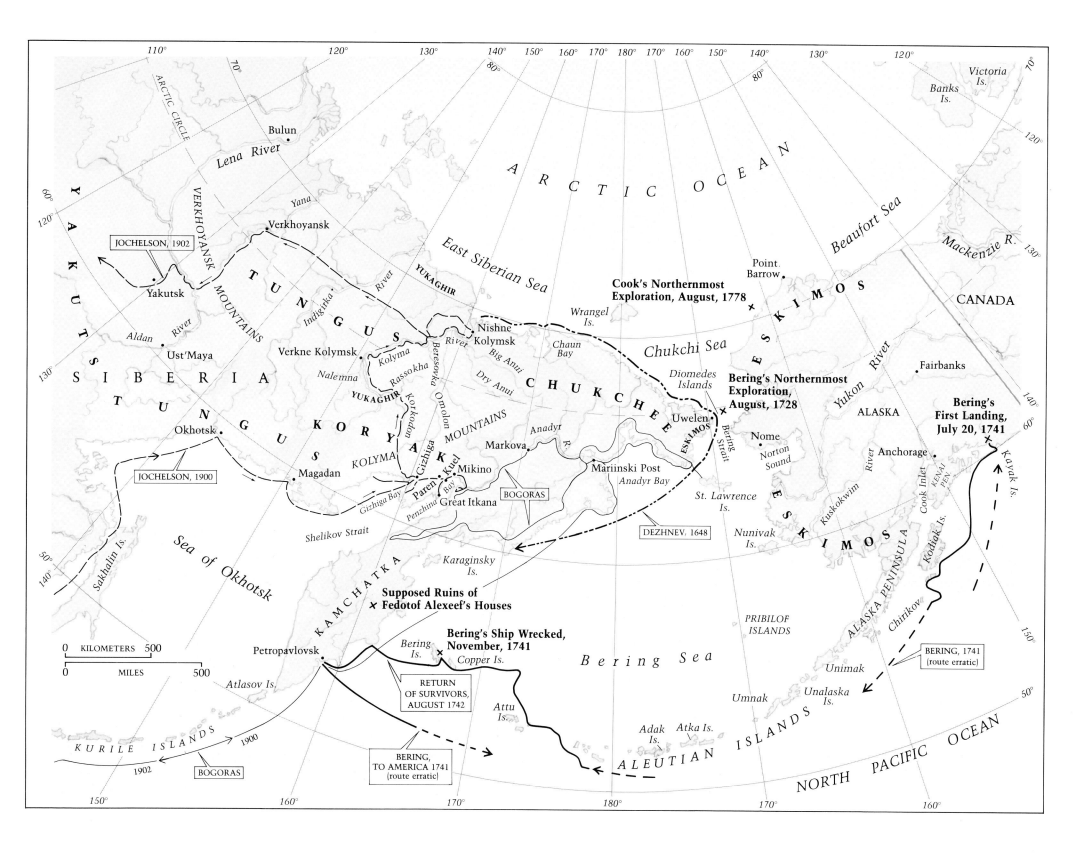

ARCTIC OCEAN

Victoria Is.

Banks Is.

ARCTIC CIRCLE

Bulun

Lena River

Yana

Verkhoyansk

Point Barrow

Cook's Northernmost Exploration, August, 1778 ×

East Siberian Sea

ESKIMOS

Beaufort Sea

Mackenzie R.

CANADA

JOCHELSON, 1902

Yakutsk

VERKHOYANSK

Indigirka

River

TUNGUS

YUKAGHIR

Wrangel Is.

Nishne Kolymsk

Chaun Bay

Chukchi Sea

Bering's Northernmost Exploration, August, 1728 ×

Fairbanks

Yukon River

ALASKA

Aldan

River

Ust'Maya

S I B E R I A

Verkne Kolymsk

Kolyma

Nalemna

Rassokha

YUKAGHIR

Beresovka

River

Big Anui

Dry Anui

C H U K C H E E

Diomedes Islands

Uwelen

ESKIMOS

Bering Strait

Nome

Norton Sound

Bering's First Landing, July 20, 1741 ×

Kayak Is.

T U N G U S

Okhotsk

Korkodon

KORYAK

Omolon

MOUNTAINS

KOLYMA

Gizhiga

Anadyr

Markova

Anadyr R.

ESKIMOS

St. Lawrence Is.

Anchorage

River

Kuskokwim

KENAI PEN.

JOCHELSON, 1900

Magadan

Paren

Kuel

Mikino

Great Itkana

BOGORAS

Mariinski Post

Anadyr Bay

Cook Inlet

Kodiak Is.

Gizhiga Bay

Penzhina Bay

Shelikov Strait

DEZHNEV, 1648

Nunivak Is.

Chirikov

ALASKA PENINSULA

Sea of Okhotsk

Karaginsky Is.

Supposed Ruins of Fedotof Alexeef's Houses ×

PRIBILOF ISLANDS

BERING, 1741 (route erratic)

Sakhalin Is.

K A M C H A T K A

Bering Is.

Bering's Ship Wrecked, November, 1741 ×

Copper Is.

Bering Sea

Unimak

| 0   KILOMETERS   500 |
| 0   MILES   500 |

Petropavlovsk

RETURN OF SURVIVORS, AUGUST 1742

Umnak

Unalaska Is.

Atlasov Is.

Attu Is.

Adak Is.

Atka Is.

A L E U T I A N   I S L A N D S

K U R I L E   I S L A N D S

1900

1902

BOGORAS

BERING, TO AMERICA 1741 (route erratic)

NORTH PACIFIC OCEAN

Y A K U T S T U N G U S

I conjecture that the new world is not altogether severed and disjoyned from the other.

—José de Acosta, *Natural and Moral History of the Indies*, 1588

Only a narrow strait separates Asia from America. Russians passing through Siberia reached the shores of this strait in 1648, but they did not learn what was on the other side. In 1728, Vitus Bering's two ships sailed into the strait, which was later named for him, but the weather was bad and he never saw America. Finally, in 1778, Captain James Cook's ships sailed through the strait, and his men returned with the news that on a clear day the New World was visible from the Old.

Once it was known that the two continents were almost joined, the question naturally arose: Was America originally peopled from Asia? In 1897, the Jesup North Pacific Expedition was formed to seek the answer. Morris K. Jesup, a New York banker and president of the American Museum of Natural History, sponsored the expedition. Franz Boas, a young anthropologist at the Museum, was its head. The plan called for an investigation of the native tribes on both sides of Bering Strait to see if they were related. From this Boas hoped to deduce how and when people might have passed between the two continents.

Much of the research of the Jesup expedition was conducted in eastern Siberia. At least half of this land is covered with trees, mostly low and stunted, but in places tall and majestic. Perhaps a quarter is treeless steppes and morasses. The rest is tundra, which stretches in a two hundred-mile-wide belt across the northern edge and down the Pacific shore to the peninsula of Kamchatka, above Japan.

In camps like the one pictured here lived the now-vanished Yukaghir. It is mid-September. Winter is about to begin. The larches have dropped their needles. Weirs have been set with the current to catch the whitefish that return to the Arctic Ocean before the rivers freeze, which happens here by the first week in October.

▶▶▶ *'The mouth of the Rassokha, a tributary of the Korkodon.' Eastern Siberia; ca. 1895. Waldemar Jochelson, photographer. Jochelson's white tent is pitched among the tents of a Yukaghir camp. Photograph courtesy of The American Museum of Natural History.*

We hope the expedition, when carried out,
will assist you in obtaining a satisfactory station in life.

—Franz Boas to Waldemar Jochelson, 1899

In the field of anthropology, nothing the size of the Jesup North Pacific Expedition had ever been organized before. Boas hired eight scientists to study the tribes on the American coasts, and four others to work on the Asiatic side. Each was provided with assistants, equipment, diplomatic permits, and funds, and assigned to his own region; so in all, there were actually twelve expeditions that covered an area stretching from northernmost Japan through Siberia and Alaska into the Canadian Northwest.

For the study of the tribes in northeast Siberia, Boas found Waldemar Jochelson. Jochelson was born in Lithuania in 1855 and educated in Russia, where he was arrested when he was thirty as a member of a revolutionary society. He spent three years in solitary confinement. Then, by order of the czar, he was exiled to northeast Siberia for ten years. There, like many political exiles, he was free to move about. He began studying the native tribes, and worked on a Russian Geographical Society expedition while still serving his term in exile. Boas met him in 1899, after he had returned from Siberia, and hired him for three-and-a-half years.

Since Jochelson could not cover all the tribes in northeast Siberia by himself, Boas hired a second researcher, Waldemar Bogoras. Bogoras was born near Kiev in 1865. He too had been a member of a revolutionary society in his university days, for which he had been jailed and exiled to Siberia. There he and Jochelson met and became friends.

From the time Jochelson and Bogoras arrived back in Siberia in the summer of 1900, they were always on the move. "The ethnographer in those polar regions," Jochelson wrote to Boas, "has to constantly search for subjects because of their small numbers, low density, and wandering." Bogoras went among his subjects on foot or by dog sledge. Jochelson traveled by reindeer and dog sledge, horse, log raft, skin boat, stagecoach, steamer, and railroad. For five days he and his party rode in the wooden boat pictured here while the collections followed by pack mule. When they were still forty miles from their destination—a town of eight houses and a church—the river froze and they had to continue on foot.

▸▸▸ *Eastern Siberia, upper Kolyma River; early October 1901. Waldemar Jochelson, photographer. At the right sits Dr. Dina Brodsky, Jochelson's wife. She accompanied her husband as a paid assistant, making anthropometric measurements and developing the negatives for all of Jochelson's photographs. Photograph courtesy of The American Museum of Natural History.*

For eight months of every year there is frost unbearable, and in these you
shall not make mud by pouring out water but by lighting a fire.

—Herodotus' description of Siberia, fifth century B.C.

"No clothing, no matter of what kind, is any protection from the cold," wrote Jochelson of the winter storms on the coasts of eastern Siberia. "Snow-flakes as fine as sand and as hard as crystals whirl through the air, creep up under the clothes, blind the eyes and cut the face. Not a thing can be seen. When I went to make observations at my weather station (which was only a few meters distant from the house), not less than three of us would venture out together, for it was very easy to be thrown down by the wind, and buried under the snow, in the very midst of a settlement.

"When a snow-storm begins to rage, the dogs are let loose in order to give them freedom to find a sheltered place for themselves. They lie down huddled together, and do not move until the falling snow makes breathing difficult. Then they get up, shake off the snow, and lie down again. In this struggle with the storm the dogs get so tired out that they lie motionless for an entire day after the storm has passed over. Dogs which are left tied perish oftentimes. When Mr. Bogoras came to visit, his driver left his dogs tied over night.

On the following morning the dogs had to be dug out from under the snow, and one of them was smothered."

Inland, the Siberian winters are quieter. Storms are rare, precipitation is light, so that the land is really a polar desert, and the still air retains less heat than anywhere else except Antarctica. Few sounds are heard except the splitting of trees and cracking of the ground by the frost. "The reindeer crowd together as closely as possible," noted Wrangell, a nineteenth-century Russian explorer, and "stand motionless, as if deprived of life. Only the raven still cleaves the icy air, leaving behind him a long line of thin vapour, marking the trail of his solitary flight."

➤➤➤ *'Burning a Koryak child's body.' Eastern Siberia; 1900. Waldemar Jochelson, photographer. Photograph courtesy of The American Museum of Natural History.*

It took me so long to learn this song, and this thing has learned it at once
without making any mistakes!

—Young Gilyak woman whose voice was recorded by the Jesup expedition

"I asked them once for a suit of clothes of a poor man," wrote Bogoras to Boas. He was collecting objects from the Chukchee that would illustrate their culture. "That was very imprudently spoken," he continued, "since now all poor men bring to me some cast-off rags to try to sell them for the most they could get. Of course they think me raving mad, since I pay for such trash with good things like brick-tea, leaf-tobacco, very hard rye-biscuit, and other delicacies. But they are very quick in taking a clue to my askings and now are very eloquent in praising their own articles. 'Look here—how beautiful it is,' says for instance some old hag, showing me a small bag of deer skin, black of dirt, with two score holes in it. 'Old, very old, really good for nothing, rotten through and through! take it and pay heavily!' "

The coastal Koryak called Jochelson "tales chief" because he recorded their tales. He used a phonograph with wax cylinders. "It made the most striking impression wherever we went," he wrote. "Often a hundred persons would crowd into the house where we put it up and gather around it in a ring. Some of the lads watched the phonograph in action with an interest as intense as if they were about to penetrate the mystery of the box which could utter words and sounds.

"The grown-up people explained it very simply, thus: 'A living being, capable of imitating humans, is sitting in the box.' They called it the 'old man.' Naturally, they were especially pleased to hear the box repeat Koryak tales and songs. But often the old people stopped the young from singing into the phonograph, saying that the 'old one' would take away their voices."

▶▶▶ *'Koryak boy with bow.' Eastern Siberia; 1901. Waldemar Jochelson, photographer. The boy wears a reindeer-hide tunic, fur side in, with a dogskin collar. In colder weather, another tunic would be added, fur side out. An American who traveled among the Reindeer Koryak in the late nineteenth century tells of them wearing "wolfskin hoods with the ears of the animal standing erect on each side of the head." Photograph courtesy of The American Museum of Natural History.*

We shudder to find man also settled here!

—Adelbert von Chamisso, 1821

Late in the Ice Age people had already come to eastern Siberia, where they hunted mammoths and horses on what were then arid polar steppes. When the glaciers retreated around 9000 B.C. and the steppes gave way to the present forests and tundras, the people hunted moose and reindeer. By 1000 B.C. they had settled stretches of the coast to hunt sea mammals.

Jochelson and Bogoras found three groups of people living in eastern Siberia. First there were the tribes that they judged to be descended from the ancient inhabitants. These included the Yukaghir and Koryak, which Jochelson studied, and the Chukchee, studied by Bogoras. The Yukaghir were inland fishermen and hunters of moose and reindeer. The Koryak and Chukchee each had a coastal branch that hunted sea mammals and an inland branch that bred reindeer. None of the tribes in this first group could work metal when the Russians confronted them early in the seventeenth century.

The second group was the Siberian Eskimos, who hunted sea mammals with stone-tipped weapons and spoke the same language as the American Eskimos. Now they live in a few villages on the shores of the Bering Sea, but once they were widespread along the Arctic and Pacific coasts of eastern Siberia, where their culture probably originated.

The third group was the Tungus, reindeer-riding hunters who still dwell throughout the forests of eastern Siberia and speak a Manchurian language. When the Russians first encountered them they were forging crude iron tools. Like the Mongols, the Tungus came from the forests north of the central Asian steppes. There, where horses will not thrive, they adopted reindeer riding, which extended the range of their hunts. They spread north into the lands of the Yukaghir, Chukchee, and Koryak, beginning in the first centuries A.D. Deprived of their game, some Yukaghir were pushed into poorer lands; others were forced to fish in the rivers and lakes, an occupation regarded by all Siberian tribes as the resort of the poor.

The Koryak and Chukchee learned from the example of the Tungus to keep half-wild reindeer, but never to ride them. Both tribes prospered more as herders than they had as hunters. In the few centuries before the Russian contact, the Chukchee were able to expand into the territory of the Yukaghir to the west and of the Eskimos to the east. Jochelson reported seeing ruined Yukaghir houses in what is today Chukchee territory. According to Bogoras, Chukchee tales mention battles in which the Siberian Eskimos were forced to flee across the sea. Today, many of the Chukchee coastal villages still bear Eskimo names.

▸▸▸ *'Wandering Tungus on reindeer back.' Eastern Siberia, probably near Gizhiga Bay, Sea of Okhotsk; June 1901. Waldemar Jochelson, photographer. Jochelson noted that the varied degree of domestication among Siberian reindeer was shown by the fact that when wolves were near, the reindeer of the Tungus ran towards their masters' tents while those of the Koryak and Chukchee scattered. Photograph courtesy of The American Museum of Natural History.*

Yukaghir campfires were as many as stars in the sky; birds which flew over them changed their color in the smoke from white to yellow.

—Traditional

The conquest of Siberia began in 1581 when Russian soldiers crossed the Urals and attacked a Moslem khanate in the Ob basin. Russian cannon defeated the warriors of the khan, who were armed with bows. Their country was annexed by Russia, and a tribute of 200,000 sable pelts was sent yearly to the czar. The Russians then advanced eastward across Siberia, reaching the Pacific Ocean sixty years later. The scattered hunting tribes they met on the way were subdued and forced to pay fur tributes. Only the Chukchee kept their independence. As a result, they continued to expand at a time when the other Siberian tribes were shrinking under Russian domination.

"Of all the tribes of northeast Siberia who have come in contact with the Russians," wrote Jochelson, "the Yukaghir have fared the worst." In the 1790s an English explorer observed, "Wars have swept off great numbers, the small-pox still more, and venereal disease now seems engrafted upon them, as if to finally eradicate the race."

To add to their woes, around 1820 the migration of wild reindeer across the eastern tributaries of the lower Kolyma "began to lessen, and finally ceased altogether," Bogoras related. "The old people of the tribe attributed this calamity to the increase of sinfulness in the world. Up to a late period, when reindeer-herds or salmon-shoals were not forthcoming, it was considered by the old people as a just punishment for the reckless extermination of game."

According to Bogoras, "The real reason the reindeer ceased to migrate probably lies in the fact that the reindeer-breeding Chukchee spread to the west, occupying the tundra pastures" with their herds of domestic deer. The Yukaghir, weakened by the Russian contact, could not defend their hunting grounds. "And so there was no place left for the wild reindeer. Yukaghir villages which depended on them for their subsistence were starved out in consequence."

▶▶▶ *'Yukaghir wandering family on the Korkodon River.' Eastern Siberia; ca. 1896. Waldemar Jochelson, photographer. The people on the right carry fish nets, which they will set through holes in the river ice. In eastern Siberia, the ice gets to be six feet thick. "When you want to pierce ice that thick," wrote Bogoras, "you have to cut with an ice pick a round funnel three meters in diameter. The working person will gradually sink down and then completely go under the surface of the ice; only the upper portion of his ice pick will be seen. Even when cut through, the hole must be pierced anew twice a day." Photograph courtesy of The American Museum of Natural History.*

> The Chukchee, a most ferocious and bellicose nation, enemies of the
> Russians, who, when captured, kill each other.
>
> —Eighteenth-century Italian map of Siberia

"When the Russians first came, our people were very much afraid of them, because they were of quite unknown appearance," Chukchee tales relate. "Their whiskers stood out like those of the walrus. All their clothing was of iron. They dug the ground with the butt-ends of their spears, like angry reindeer-bucks, inviting our warriors to single combat."

But later the Chukchee began to raid the Russian fur caravans and outposts. In retaliation, the Russians sent a military expedition, led by Theodore Pavlutsky, against them in 1729. Pavlutsky fought the Chukchee for seventeen years. He killed many of them, including women and children, but he could not break their resistance.

In March 1747, according to accounts compiled by Bogoras from Siberian archives, "Pavlutsky went in pursuit of a large Chukchee party. He bade the main body of his soldiers to follow behind, and he himself went forward, having with him only eighty men. Soon he overtook the enemy, who were very numerous, standing on the hill. The Russians held a council. One lieutenant proposed to wait for the other party; but the other lieutenant said angrily, 'It seems that our Cossacks are war-like only at home, and in battle they are weak-hearted. The present is the time to strike the enemy.' So they rushed onward, but a part of the Chukchee caught them from behind. Some of the Cossacks fled on reindeer sledges, and escaped. Others fought, but were killed.

"Pavlutsky was wounded and fell to the ground; but the Chukchee for a long time could find no place in his armor through which to deal a mortal blow. Chukchee tradition says that he was wounded in the right eye, then killed with a knife thrust into the abdomen under a joint of the armor. So he died." Another historian adds, "For many years after the Chukchee kept his head for a trophy."

"The expedition of Pavlutsky was the last military enterprise of the Russians against the Chukchee," Bogoras continued. Thereafter, "intercourse with them, renewed in 1789, was carried on with much circumspection. No new attempt was made to conquer the Chukchee by force, and up to the present time [1904], there are many camps and villages where a Russian face has never been seen, nor a word of the Russian language heard."

▸▸▸ *'Yukaghir summer village on the Korkodon River.' Eastern Siberia; ca. 1895. Waldemar Jochelson, photographer. Photograph courtesy of The American Museum of Natural History.*

George Kennan, an American engineer surveying in Siberia in the 1860s, lived in Koryak houses one winter. "They have not one redeeming feature," he wrote. "They are entered through the chimney, lighted by the chimney, and ventilated by the chimney; the sunshine falls into them once a year—in June; they are cold in winter, close and uncomfortable in summer, and smoky all the time."

But to Jochelson they were better than any alternative. Once in a Koryak village, he related, "my wife and I occupied a small Russian log-cabin belonging to a cossack who was absent at that time. Every wind, violent or not, would cover our house with snow to the top, and we were fastened in until my men (a cossack and an interpreter), who slept in a neighboring Koryak house, came, together with Koryaks, and cleared away the snow from our door."

Kennan wrote that "when snow drifts up against the houses so as to give the dogs access to the chimney, they take a perfect delight in lying around the hole, peering down and snuffing the odours of boiling fish which rise from the huge kettle underneath. Not unfrequently they get into a grand comprehensive free fight for the best place of observation; and just as you are about to take your dinner of boiled salmon off the fire, down comes a struggling, yelping dog into the kettle, while his triumphant antagonist looks down through the chimney hole with all the complacency of gratified vengeance upon his unfortunate victim. A Koryak takes the half-scalded dog by the back of the neck, carries him up the chimney, pitches him over the edge of the roof into a snow-drift, and returns with unruffled serenity to eat the fish-soup which has thus been irregularly flavoured with dog and thickened with hairs."

▶▶▶ *Interior of semi-subterranean house at Mikino, a village of the Maritime Koryak tribe, on the northern shore of the Sea of Okhotsk, eastern Siberia; 1900. Waldemar Jochelson, photographer. The ladder leads to the winter entrance at the top of the roof. "Occasionally a Koryak falls from the ladder," Jochelson wrote, "but as a rule they run up the ladder, their children on their backs, with heavy buckets of water, or with pails filled with hot soup for the dogs. The ladder is the master of the house entrance. Its top, which has a crudely carved human face, and its foot are smeared with fat and charmed by means of an incantation, in order that the ladder may not admit evil spirits or ill-meaning people into the house." Photograph courtesy of The American Museum of Natural History.*

There was much praying, to be sure, but the curses piled up during ten years
in Siberia prevented any response.

—Georg Steller, 1741

On June 6, 1741, Vitus Bering sailed from Kamchatka, after ten years of preparation, in his second attempt to reach America. After forty days at sea, he sighted the coast of southern Alaska. While his crew rejoiced, Bering was cautious: "We think now we have accomplished everything, and may go about greatly inflated, but they do not consider how far we are from home, and what may yet happen." They landed just long enough to take on fresh water, then started on their return voyage the next morning. "We had come only for the purpose of bringing American water to Asia," commented Georg Steller, the ship's naturalist.

On the passage back they sailed for three-and-a-half months through almost continuous headwinds and storms. Scurvy broke out. "Half our crew lay sick; the other half were of necessity able-bodied but quite crazed and maddened from the terrifying motion of the sea and ship," wrote Steller. On November 4 they sighted land. "God knows whether this is Kamchatka," Steller exclaimed. "What else can it be?" answered the navigator. But when they anchored, sea otters, which in Kamchatka were made shy and rare by constant hunting, swam out to the ship as if to greet them. And when Steller went ashore, blue foxes, likewise persecuted in Kamchatka, gathered about them in countless numbers. The foxes mutilated their dead before they could be buried, and even dared to attack the living.

On November 28, during a snowstorm, the anchored ship was driven ashore and wrecked. Bering died from scurvy on December 8. On Christmas Eve an exploring party returned with the news that they were on a treeless island and that from the other side the volcanoes of Kamchatka were visible at times. The survivors spent the winter in pits that they dug and covered with sails. For food, they killed foxes, sea otters, and animals they called sea cows that no one had seen before.

The next summer they built a new ship from the wreckage of the old. They boarded it on August 13, and "watched the foxes on shore ransacking our dwellings and occupying them as living quarters," wrote Steller. The voyagers arrived in Kamchatka on August 27, after rowing several days against the wind. "We had been regarded by everybody as dead," Steller related. "The property which we had left behind had fallen into the hands of strangers and had been carried away." Forty-five of the original seventy-seven returned. The island where they were shipwrecked was named for Bering.

▶▶▶ *'Post boat, Lena River.' Central Siberia; 1897. Waldemar Jochelson, photographer. There, in the thick forests on the far upper reaches of the Lena River, tigers were occasionally killed as late as the 1820s, according to Alexander von Humboldt. For a few weeks each June, at the time of the thaw, the Lena carries more water than any other river on earth. Photograph courtesy of The American Museum of Natural History.*

It was therefore already decided that there was no connection between the two parts of the world; but this had been forgotten.

—Gerhard Müller, alluding to Dezhnev's voyage, knowledge of which
had been lost until Müller found the original reports
in a Siberian archive in 1736

The first person to determine the eastward extent of Siberia was the Cossack Simon Dezhnev. He was second in command of a party of about three hundred Russians that left the mouth of the Kolyma River in seven boats in June 1648. The boats sailed east through the Arctic Ocean to Bering Strait, and then south into the Pacific. There they were separated. Dezhnev's boat, with twenty-four men, was driven ashore on the Siberian coast. He and twelve others survived and returned overland to the Kolyma seven years later.

The fates of the commander of the expedition, Fedot Alexeef, and the rest of the people are not known for certain. However, Dezhnev reported that on his way home he "captured from the Koryaks a Yakut woman who had been on the ship of Fedot Alexeef, and she said that Fedot died of scurvy, some of his companions were killed [by the Koryak], and the few who remained escaped in boats with their lives, and she did not know what become of them."

Of those few who escaped, historians report that when Russian Cossacks in 1697 "first attempted the reduction of Kamchatka, they found that the inhabitants had previous knowledge of the Russians. A common tradition still prevails that a certain Fedotof, most likely a son of Fedot

Alexeef, and his companions had resided amongst them, and intermarried with the natives. They even point to the spot where the Russians had their homes. They are said to have been held in great veneration, and almost worshipped by the inhabitants, who at first imagined that no human power could hurt them; until they fought amongst themselves, and the blood was seen to flow from their wounds," at which time the Kamchatkans "were glad to rid themselves of such dangerous neighbors."

▸▸▸ *'A Yakut blacksmith who has established himself under the roof of a sledge shed belonging to a rich Yakut patron.' Eastern Siberia, summer 1902. Waldemar Jochelson, photographer. The Yakuts are a Turkic-speaking people from the steppes of Central Asia. They raise cattle and horses on the meadows and tundras of Siberia, where they moved in about the fourteenth century after the steppes were conquered from their ancestors by the Mongols. In their customs and language, the Yakuts resemble steppe tribes from whom they are separated by a forest belt 500 miles wide. In their poetry they still speak of camels and apple orchards, and the months of their calendar are still named for events, such as ice-breaking and haymaking, that occur much later in their present home. Photograph courtesy of The American Museum of Natural History.*

> The scene was indescribably ghastly and desolate, though laid in a country
> purified by frost as if by fire.
>
> —John Muir, Saint Lawrence Island, 1881

In July 1881, the U.S.S. *Corwin* visited Saint Lawrence Island, off the coast of eastern Siberia, to investigate reports of famine there among the Eskimo inhabitants in the winter of 1879–80. "I landed at a village where there were 200 dead people," wrote Edward W. Nelson, a Smithsonian Institution anthropologist. "In a large house were found about fifteen bodies placed one upon another like cordwood at one end of the room, while as many others lay dead on their blankets on the platforms." C. L. Hooper, the *Corwin*'s captain, reported that the famine had claimed "not less than a thousand lives out of a population of less than fifteen hundred. The percentage of deaths was so extraordinary that I have at times thought that the island must have been visited by an epidemic. But the invariable answer of the survivors when asked the cause was, 'No get eat,' and no amount of cross-questioning could elicit any other."

According to Nelson, "this terrible famine was said to be caused by the use of whiskey. The people of that island usually obtained their supply of food for the winter by killing walrus from the great herds of these animals that go through Bering Strait on the first ice in the fall. The walrus remain about the island only a few days and then go south, when the ice closes about and shuts the island in till spring.

"Just before the time for the walrus to reach the island that season, the Eskimo obtained a supply of whiskey from some vessels and began a prolonged debauch, which ended only when the supply was exhausted. When this occurred the annual migration of walrus had passed, and people were shut in for the winter by the ice. The result was that over two-thirds of the population died before spring."

There is, however, the possibility that the Eskimos were drunk because they had missed the walrus hunt. Hooper observed that the Saint Lawrence Eskimos "subsist almost entirely upon seals and walrus, which they take during the winter at or near the edge of the ice and at the holes which open up as the ice breaks and changes its position. When the ice remains unbroken a long distance from the shore and thick, stormy weather prevails, so that the natives cannot hunt, their supply of food is cut off. This seems to have been the case during the winter of 1879–80, judging from native accounts." Bogoras heard that in 1879, "famine ravaged the whole coast from Anadyr to Bering Straits, St. Lawrence Island included."

▸▸▸ *Great Itkana, a village of the Maritime Koryak tribe on Penzhina Bay, Sea of Okhotsk, eastern Siberia; 1900. Waldemar Jochelson, photographer. The dome-shaped semi-subterranean log house of the Maritime Koryak is a type commonly used by northern peoples of both hemispheres. The Koryak version is often surmounted by a funnel-shaped structure. "This funnel," Jochelson explained, "is built for the purpose of protecting the upper entrance to the underground house from drifting snow piled up by the raging winter storms. The snow driven by the gale from any point of the compass strikes against the lower part of the funnel and is scattered in all directions." Photograph courtesy of The American Museum of Natural History.*

We are surrounded by enemies. Spirits always walk about invisibly with
gaping mouths. We are always cringing, and distributing gifts on all sides,
asking protection from one, giving ransom to another.

—Chukchee shaman, ca. 1895

The spirits of various diseases come "mostly from the west, out of the country of the Big Sun Chief [the czar]," Bogoras was told by a Chukchee shaman, or priest. "Sometimes these [evil spirits] appear in visible form, as animals," the Koryak, whose beliefs are much the same as the Chukchee's, told Jochelson. "Some Koryak," he wrote, "in speaking about the epidemic of measles of 1900, which exterminated a considerable number of the inhabitants of the Gizhiga district, told me that the spirits which caused the epidemic came running from the direction of the sunset in the guise of colts. This particular idea can be explained by the fact that the measles had been brought to the country by the Russians, hence the spirits of that disease assumed the form of a Russian animal."

Jochelson related that in March 1901 he had rented twenty sledges in Paren, a Koryak village, for the purpose of carrying his collection to the Russian settlement of Gizhiginsk. When Jochelson reached Gizhiginsk, he dismissed the Paren drivers and they went home. "A month later," he continued, "I again passed through Paren, and was surprised at the number of dog-sacrifices which I found hanging there. All along the bank of the Paren River were stakes driven into the snow, with dogs hanging on them, their muzzles pointing upward. In the light of the spring sun, this long row of dog-sacrifices offered a queer and sad sight.

"I found out that the greater part of the dogs had been killed by the drivers of the sledges which I had hired in gratitude for their safe return from Gizhiginsk, and to guard their villages against the spirit of measles, which a year previous had come to them from that little town."

▸▸▸ *Sacrificed dogs at Paren, a village of the Maritime Koryak on the shore of Penzhina Bay, Sea of Okhotsk, eastern Siberia; April 1901. Waldemar Jochelson, photographer. Photograph courtesy of The American Museum of Natural History.*

All that exists, lives. The walls of the house have voices of their own. The antlers lying on the tombs arise at night and walk in procession around the mound, while the deceased rise and visit the living.

—Chukchee shaman, ca. 1895

"In memory of their shaman-ancestors the ancient Yukaghir used to hang representations of human figures on trees," wrote Jochelson. "These were called cancaromo, which means 'wooden man.' In the wooden man dwelled the spirit of the deceased, and it was addressed as the ancestor.

"One such wooden man was pointed out to me. It was suspended from an old larch tree standing on a cliff called Shaman's Stone, which is situated on the high bank of the Kolyma River. It was very crude, made of a log about five feet long. The mouth was indicated by a deep line. The eyes consisted of two holes in which two stones were stuck. The trunk was split to indicate the feet.

"I decided to take the figure with me. But I deemed it wise not to reveal my intention to my Yukaghir guides until we crossed the Kolyma River towards the cliff on which the idol was suspended. Then I told them. 'You are taking it yourself. We are not giving it to you,' said their chief. 'Our ancestor will, of course, be angry, but we have nothing to do with it.' He threw offerings into the fire and said half-jokingly, half-seriously: 'Grandfather, the Russian wants to carry you away. With good thoughts go.'

"When I brought the wooden man to the Yukaghir village, some of the women went into nervous fits. In a few days a young Yukaghir returned from the hunt and told that while in the woods and, as he pretended, without knowing that I brought the wooden man with me, he had the follow-ing dream. A man in silver garments came to him and said, 'I am your ancestor. Nine generations did not molest me, respected me; now I am being taken away no one knows where; get up and tell all, that the one who first pointed me out, the one who took me down and the one who carries me off, all shall suffer.'

"I tried to calm them, tried to persuade them that the grandfather will fare better with us than with them, that he will hang under glass in a warm room of a large royal house, that he will be fed, and that people will come to look at him as well as on other wooden men who hang there. Unfortunately, this wooden man was not destined to reach the museum. When my collection arrived at Yakutsk, the idol was not there."

▶▶▶ *'Three masked persons pretending to warm themselves by a wood-pile.' Koryak village of Paren, Penzhina Bay, eastern Siberia; December 1900. Waldemar Jochelson, photographer. "In Paren," wrote Jochelson, "masks are worn to drive away the kalau [evil spirits] who have taken possession of the houses during the absence of the people in summer. Only the young men wore masks. They rolled down into the house with great noise, missing several steps of the ladder. They examined all the nooks and corners. Then they commenced a dance, and represented various scenes of the coming winter life. Thus they visited all the houses." Photograph courtesy of The American Museum of Natural History.*

From the time when we began hunting the sea cow we were not in want.

—Lieutenant Yushin Khitrov, with Bering, 1742

When Bering and his men were shipwrecked on their way home from America in 1741, some of them thought they had reached Kamchatka. But Steller doubted it, "since I saw the many Manati, which I had never before seen and which were known nowhere in Kamchatka." Indeed, these "Manati," since named Steller's sea cows, existed only in the waters around Bering Island, where the men were wrecked, and nearby Copper Island.

Steller's sea cow (*Rhytina stelleri*) was the sole northern form of an order that includes the manatees and dugongs of tropical waters. It was about thirty feet long, black, and shaped something like a tadpole, with short forelegs, a round belly, and a tapering tail ending in horizontal flukes. According to Steller, it had a head like a buffalo, a hide like an ancient oak, a back like an ox, breasts like a human, and feet like a horse. Instead of teeth it had two "white bones or solid tooth masses." The stomach was "of stupendous size, six feet long, and five feet wide"; the intestines, six inches in diameter and almost five hundred feet long.

"These animals, like cattle, live in herds at sea, males and females going together and driving the young before them," wrote Steller. "They are occupied with nothing else but their food. The back and half the body are always seen out of water. They tear seaweed from the rocks with the feet and chew it without cessation. During the eating they move the head and neck like an ox, and after the lapse of a few minutes they lift the head out of the water, and draw fresh air with a rasping and snorting sound after the manner of horses.

"After the supplying of provisions began to become difficult because of the frightening away of the sea otters," Steller continued, "we considered ways to secure these [sea cows]." They soon found they could strike a sea cow with a harpoon attached to a heavy cable held by thirty men and slowly draw it to shore. Steller noted that "when one of them was hooked, all the others were intent upon saving him. Some tried to prevent the wounded comrade from being drawn to the beach by forming a closed circle around him; some attempted to upset the yawl, others laid themselves over the rope or tried to pull the harpoon out of his body, in which indeed they succeeded several times. We also noticed that a male came two days in succession to its female which was lying dead on the beach. Nevertheless, no matter how many of them were wounded or killed they always remained in one place."

Following Bering's expedition, Russians began sailing to the Aleutians to hunt for furs. Sea-cow meat, salted down while they wintered on Bering and Copper Islands, was their main provision. By 1755, this practice had driven the sea cows from Copper Island. "The last of this species was killed on Bering's Island in 1768," wrote a nineteenth-century explorer, "and none have been ever seen since."

▶▶▶ *'The inhabitants of Kuel haul a white whale* [Delphinapterus leucas] *caught in seal-nets on dog-sleds over the coast-ice to the settlement.' Eastern Siberia, east coast of Penzhina Bay, Sea of Okhotsk; October 1900. Waldemar Jochelson, photographer. Photograph courtesy of The American Museum of Natural History.*

The places of sea and land change,
and there is no place on earth always land nor always sea.

—El-Mas'udi, Arabic geographer, A.D. 950

The ringed seal (*Phoca hispida*) lives in the Arctic Ocean and adjacent waters. A near relative, the Baikal seal (*Phoca sibirica*), lives only in Lake Baikal, high in the mountains of Central Asia, two thousand miles from the Arctic Ocean.

How seals got to Lake Baikal has long puzzled scientists. Peter Simon Pallas, an eighteenth-century German naturalist in Siberia, commented, "I cannot help thinking these animals were left in those Lakes ever since the Deluge which passed over the continent of Asia." But geologists are almost certain there has not been a global flood since the time that seals appeared on earth.

The seals probably got to Lake Baikal during the Ice Age. It is likely that then as now, they lived in the great bays in the western Siberian plain that stretch down from the Arctic Ocean to meet the north-flowing rivers, and that they followed the shoals of fish that migrated back and forth from the rivers to the ocean. During the Ice Age, glaciers flowed out onto the northern part of the plain from the mountains on either side. The ice sheets cut across the bays, blocked the flow of the rivers to the ocean, and trapped the seals and fish behind them. The waters of the rivers backed up and collected to form a huge temporary lake, in which generations of seals lived.

The level of the temporary lake rose until its arms brought the seals to a point within six hundred miles of Lake Baikal. The large river that drains Lake Baikal flowed into this lake. Although Baikal today is about a thousand feet higher than the temporary glacial lake was, during the Ice Age its waters were lower and fell from it less precipitously, making it possible for both seals and fish to swim up to it from the lake below.

Ringed seals and their relatives are known to be great travelers. *Phoca sibirica* has been encountered in rivers thirty miles above Lake Baikal and one hundred miles below it. And Bogoras reported, "trustworthy people relate that the [ringed] seals which ascend the Anadyr after the salmon-shoals often turn into its affluents. If belated from return by river, on account of low water or early frosts, they start on a quite wonderful overland journey on impracticable roads among the hills. I was shown the skin of a seal killed on such a journey."

▶▶ *'Yukaghir women on Nalemna River.' Eastern Siberia; fall, ca. 1895. Waldemar Jochelson, photographer. They are gathering whitefish* (Coregonus migratorius), *which migrate to the Arctic Ocean when the rivers start to freeze. "The women work with the needle in the open air even in March, at a temperature of 30° below [Fahrenheit]," Bogoras observed. "Their fingers remain unprotected for several hours at a stretch. The exertion even makes them feel warm and perspire so, that they throw aside their ample fur bodices and remain half naked; or else even thrust large cakes of snow into their bosoms." Photograph courtesy of The American Museum of Natural History.*

They cover a big mountain, and nobody can count them.

—Chukchee chief, 1881, when asked how many reindeer were in his herd

"Two large migrating bodies of [wild] rein-deer passed us at no great distance," wrote Wrangell, the Russian explorer, on the Kolyma in 1822. "Both bodies of deer extended further than the eye could reach, and formed a compact mass, narrowing at the front. They moved slowly and majestically along, their broad antlers resembling a moving wood of leafless trees. Each body was led by a deer of unusual size, which my guides assured me was always a female. One of the herds was stealthily followed by a wolf, the other by a large black bear."

Wild reindeer were the staple prey of many Stone Age peoples. The hunts took place in the spring and fall, when the animals collected into herds and migrated between their summer and winter pastures. Bogoras witnessed a Chukchee reindeer hunt on the Anadyr River: "At the end of July, the reindeer begin to assemble and come back to the river. Reindeer-herds take the same trail every year, and cross the river at the same places. There the hunters lie in ambush and wait. They occupy a place a little downstream from the trail, and keep very quiet.

"The reindeer come to the river and begin to swim across. When the animals are not far from the middle of the river, the hunters rush out in canoes and boats. The frightened animals turn upstream, and exhaust their strength in a vain struggle with the force of the running water; then one or two canoes go around the herd in order to cut off their retreat, and slaughtering begins. The reindeer huddle together, and float quite helplessly in the middle of the stream. Men in canoes approach the herd and stab the reindeer with spears, which have a very long and slender shaft, a small iron point, and are not used for any other kind of hunting.

"The killing is done with incredible rapidity, a man being able to kill as many as a hundred animals in one hour. The wound is inflicted on the lower part of the body, and the wounded animals immediately turn on the side and are carried away by the stream. Most of them do not attempt defense. Young strong bucks, however, often try to kick at the canoe. Those hunters who are most skillful with the paddle penetrate into the middle of the herd, and, placing their canoe close between two large bucks, spear all the animals within reach, beginning with those farthest away; while the nearest, not being disturbed, keep quiet, and their bodies shield the canoe from the surrounding commotion. Old men, women and children row in boats farther down the river, and intercept the game. In a successful season one family will have as their share from a hundred and fifty to two hundred reindeer."

▶▶▶ *Eastern Siberia; spring 1901. Waldemar Jochelson, photographer. 'This picture,' wrote Jochelson, 'shows the camp of a not-very-wealthy Reindeer Koryak in spring. The herd, consisting of 400 reindeer, was rounded up to be moved. Between the Koryak tents my own little tent was pitched.' Reindeer eat lichens, which they get in the winter by kicking away the light snow with their forehooves. They are said to relish mice at certain times of year, and some tribes feed them dried fish. Siberian reindeer-breeders keep few dogs, since the dogs are apt to eat the deer. Nor do they have corrals. They herd the deer on foot, catch them with lassos, and keep them near by offering them human urine, to which they are strongly attracted. Photograph courtesy of The American Museum of Natural History.*

What proves, I think, that the world is a little
older than our nurses tell us are the finds of bones of elephants long ago
extinct imbedded in the ground in Northern Siberia.

—Catherine the Great to Voltaire, 1771

Coming back from Siberia in 1902, Jochelson met the Mammoth Expedition of the Imperial Russian Academy of Sciences. They were heading for the Beresovka River, a tributary of the Kolyma, where they would recover the frozen body of an extinct woolly mammoth. The carcass had been revealed when the stream bank in which it was imbedded washed away. It was nearly entire, and included even soft tissue, hair, and unchewed food in the mouth consisting of grasses that still grow in the region today. This was the best-preserved specimen found to date. But remains of mammoths had long been known in Siberia, where certain tribes believed them to be underground dwellers that had died when they came in contact with the air.

The Beresovka mammoth had apparently died from a fall. Herbert Lang, the Congo explorer, studied the evidence collected by the mammoth expedition: "The cramped position, broken bones, large amount of clotted blood in the body cavity, point towards instantaneous death by accident. The victim did not even have time to throw out the quantities of fodder between its molars." The mammoth had probably fallen into a large crack in the ground caused by frost. Water often fills these cracks, freezes on the surface, and drains away below, "giving rise to what really amounts to an underground cave, a formation not rare in Northeast-ern Siberia," Lang noted. All the ground in those parts is permanently frozen a few feet under the surface, even in summer. When the mammoth fell into the crack it was below the frost level, so that its body did not decompose during its long entombment.

Mammoth bones remain over much of the Northern Hemisphere. In eastern Siberia, fossil mammoth tusks are found often enough to form a regular item of trade (Jochelson noted that nine hundred pounds were exported from Gizhiga in 1897). These fossils come from mammoths that probably died in the annual floods that still inundate the Siberian river valleys at the time of the spring thaw. Each year, the carcasses of animals drowned by the floods are swept to the Arctic Ocean and washed into shoals, where they settle to the bottom.

▸▸▸ *'My Yukaghir guides.' Eastern Siberia; ca. 1895. Waldemar Jochelson, photographer. "Very few people are met in that region who do not use tobacco in some form," Bogoras observed. "Even children three years old, who are just toddling about, are seen smoking. Mothers give their pipes to suckling babes to quiet their crying. Scarcity of tobacco is felt as keenly as a food famine." Photograph courtesy of The American Museum of Natural History.*

> The most important of the unsolved problems in the life history of the race.
>
> —Morris K. Jesup to President McKinley, 1897

The fieldwork of the Jesup expedition was completed on the northwest coast of America in 1899; in southeast Siberia, in 1900. In eastern Siberia, Bogoras finished in 1901 and Jochelson in 1902.

The written records of each member of the expedition were edited and published by Franz Boas. Because Boas refused to cut information he believed was valuable, most of the volumes expanded beyond their planned limits. The whole series fell so far into debt that Jesup withdrew his support after 1903. From then until 1924, when the last volume came out, Boas could not get funds in advance, and had to ask his authors to do work for which he could pay them nothing until after publication. These volumes describing the tribes of the North Pacific, some of whom have since disappeared, were the most important achievement to come out of the expedition.

Boas had intended to write a volume of conclusions based on the work of the expedition. But the facts gathered raised more questions than they answered, and Boas could only say that "the Jesup Expedition seems to have established the close relationship between the peoples of Asia and America."

Jochelson spent the years 1903–1908 at the American Museum of Natural History compiling his research on the Koryak and Yukaghir. Before he had finished, he went back to Siberia to lead another expedition. After the Russian Revolution he returned to New York, completed his volumes, and died there in 1937 at the age of eighty-two. Bogoras stayed in Russia. He finished his manuscript on the Chukchee prior to serving a prison sentence for alleged complicity in the 1905 uprising. After his release, he worked as a war correspondent and became a distinguished anthropologist and novelist in Soviet Russia, where he died at the age of seventy-one in 1936.

▸▸▸ *'Reindeer teams with collections.' Central Siberia, Verkhoyansk Mountains; March or April 1902. Waldemar Jochelson, photographer. This interior country, lying near the cold pole of the Northern Hemisphere, gets very little precipitation and is virtually uninhabited. Photograph courtesy of The American Museum of Natural History.*

With what thought, with what industry, with what force did the lineage of
the Indians pass such a vast sea?

—José de Acosta, 1588

The aboriginal Americans bear a physical resemblance to the East Asians, but only in the parts of America lying nearest to Asia do they have a cultural resemblance as well. To the first modern explorers of the North Pacific, it seemed doubtful that the cultural similarities could have been due to direct contact between the tribes, so few and isolated were their settlements, so wide and stormy the seas, and so repellent the coasts. Yet when Boas compared the tribes of the American shore with those of the Asian, he found that their resemblances extended even to arbitrary details of art, weapons, and mythology. Today it is almost certain that in the North Pacific there was contact between the aboriginal Americans and Asians long after they had split apart, in a culturally unformed state, to occupy different continents.

The contact was probably by coastal voyaging. After the time of the Jesup expedition, archaeologists digging in the remains of early settlements on the North Pacific shores found traces of boats. These were commonly made of skins stretched over a wooden frame, like those still used by the Koryak, Chukchee, and Eskimos. In such boats people can venture into the sea. On Saint Lawrence Island in May 1881, an American sea captain saw an Eskimo family that had just crossed fifty miles of open sea from Siberia in a skin boat. "At that season the sea was filled with large fields of drift-ice, and subject to dense fogs, snow-storms, etc. When I asked if they were not afraid to venture so far to sea, they laughed heartily and said 'Pow' (no) with a manner that left no doubt of their entire confidence in the seaworthiness of their craft."

In skin boats, "the Chukchi not only coast along the shore," wrote an eighteenth-century explorer in Siberia, "but they very often pass Behring's strait in these, attack the habitations of the savage Americans, and, after plundering them, carry away many prisoners." Bogoras once met such a captive in Siberia. "She was an old widow of American Eskimo origin. The other women, when speaking of her, called her, with a shade of contempt, 'the slave-woman.' "

It is also possible that unplanned contacts took place directly across the breadth of the North Pacific Ocean. Just as polar bears occasionally drift on ice floes from Greenland to Iceland two hundred miles away, so have humans survived trips of more than a thousand miles on drifting ice and much farther in drifting boats. In one such case in 1833, the crew of a junk disabled off Japan drifted across the North Pacific to the coast of British Columbia, where they were cast ashore. Three of them lived. They were enslaved by the Indians until ransomed by an agent of the Hudson's Bay Company.

▸▸▸ *'Fish gate on the Nalemna River.' Eastern Siberia; fall, ca. 1895. Waldemar Jochelson, photographer. In the fall, when the fish return to the ocean after spawning, the Yukaghir build barriers of brush and sticks across the rivers into which they set gates or weirs, like the one they are standing on, where the fish are trapped. Photograph courtesy of The American Museum of Natural History.*

We are led to look to the northwestern side of North America as the former
point of communication between the Old and so-called New World.

—Charles Darwin, 1831

A broad plain, covered sparsely with grasses, brush, and lichens. Shaggy elephants. Various antelopes, bison, deer, sheep, and horses, some of giant size. Huge cats, wolves, and bears. Short warm summers, long frigid winters. On one side, mountains covered with unmelting ice; on the other, a sea covered with the same. Probably these were the surroundings of the first people to come into the New World.

The plain lay above what is now Alaska and eastern Siberia and formed a bridge between Asia and America. The animals that crossed the bridge were all adapted to the cold. People could not cross until after they had learned the use of fire and clothing and shelter. When they came, it was as hunters of the largest animals. In pursuit of their prey, they wandered first into ice-free central Alaska and the Mackenzie basin. It is likely that for a time the way farther south was barred by a glacier belt lying across central Canada.

When the glaciers began to wane, the belt parted, and the people moved southward through the gap into a New World filled with animals that had never seen a human. At about that same time, waters from the melting glaciers covered the plain between Siberia and Alaska, and drowned the traces of those who had migrated to America. Probably we can never find the remains of the closest Old World ancestors of the first New World peoples, and the search will have to be taken up by a fossil-hunting being in another age, when the land again rises above the sea.

▸▸▸ *Camp of the Reindeer Chukchee on the tundra near the mouth of the Kolyma River; eastern Siberia, 1895. Waldemar Bogoras, photographer. Photograph courtesy of The American Museum of Natural History.*

NOTES

In many of the quotations used in the text I have cut away words and altered the order of others without, I hope, changing the sense of the originals. For the sake of brevity such tailoring is not marked, but for anyone who would read the originals, the sources are noted below. All direct quotations are cited. So are statements clearly in need of reference. No citations are given for quotations taken from the photographers' picture notes. Such quotations appear only in the captions and are enclosed in single quotation marks.

THE ARCTIC

PAGE FOUR

Epigraph: John Davis, *The Worldes Hydrographical Description* (London: Thomas Dawson, 1595), C4ʳ.

Robert Thorne to King Henry VIII of England, n.d., from Richard Hakluyt, *The Principal Voyages . . . of the English Nation . . .* (London, 1598–1600), quoted in Robert Huish, *The Last Voyage of Captain Sir John Ross to the Arctic Regions . . . in the Years 1829–33* (London: John Saunders, 1835), p. 23.

Peary to President Theodore Roosevelt, n.d., quoted in Robert E. Peary, *Nearest the Pole, a narrative of the Peary Arctic Club . . . 1905–1906* (New York: Doubleday, Page & Co., 1907), introduction, p. ix.

PAGE SIX

Epigraph: Abacuk Prickett. "A Larger Discourse of the Same Voyage" (Henry Hudson's fourth, 1610), from Samuel Purchas, *Purchas His Pilgrimage . . .* (London,

1617), vol. 3, pp. 567–610, quoted in G. M. Asher, ed., *Henry Hudson the Navigator; the Original Documents in which His Career is Recorded*, Hakluyt Society Series 1, vol. 27 (London, 1860), p. 100.

Thorne, quoted in Huish, *Last Voyage of John Ross*, p. 22.

Caption: William Bradford, *The Arctic Regions* (London: Sampson Low, Marston, Low, & Searle, 1873), pl. 98.

PAGE EIGHT

Epigraph: From the Icelandic *Flateyjarbók* (ca. 1395); see *The Flatey Book and Recently Discovered Vatican Manuscripts Concerning America as Early as the 10th Century* (London: Norroena Society, 1906), p. 13.

Isaac Israel Hayes, *The Land of Desolation* (New York: Harper & Brothers, 1872), p. 39.

See also David Crantz, *The History of Greenland* (London: Brethren's Society, 1767), vol. 1, bk. 4.

Knud Rasmussen, *Across Arctic America, a Narrative of the Fifth Thule Expedition* (1927; reprint ed., New York: Greenwood Press, 1969), pp. 285–86.

Vilhjalmur Stefansson, quoted by Adophus W. Greely, "The Origin of Stefansson's Blond Eskimo," *National Geographic Magazine* (National Geographic Society, Washington, D.C.) 23 (December 1912): 1225.

PAGE TEN

Epigraph: Davis, *Worldes Hydrographical Description*, C4ᵛ.

Knud Rasmussen, *Greenland by the Polar Sea*, trans. Asta and Rowland Kenney (London: William Heinemann, 1921), p. 313.

Douglas Charles Clavering, "Journal of a Voyage to Spitzbergen and the East Coast of Greenland," *The Edinburgh New Philosophical Journal* (Adam Black, Edinburgh) 9 (1830): 24.

Helge Larson, "Dodemandsbugten, an Eskimo Settlement on Clavering Island," *Meddelelser om Grønland* (C. A. Reitzel, Copenhagen) 102, no. 1 (1934): 163–70.

Rasmussen, *Greenland*, pp. 315, 317.

PAGE TWELVE

Epigraph: Sir John Ross, *Narrative of a Second Voyage in Search of a North-west Passage . . . During the Years 1829–33* (Philadelphia: E. L. Carey & A. Hart, 1835), p. 145.

George F. Lyon, *The Private Journal of Captain G. F. Lyon of HMS. Hecla During the Recent Voyage of Discovery Under Captain Parry 1821–23* (1824; reprint ed., Barre, Mass.: Imprint Society, 1970), p. 115.

Peary, *Nearest the Pole* , p. 388.

Caption: Elisha Kent Kane, *Arctic Explorations: The Second Grinnell Expedition in Search of Sir John Franklin, 1853, 1854, 1855* (Philadelphia: Childs & Peterson, 1857), p. 203.

PAGE FOURTEEN

Epigraph: John Cabot, quoted in Huish, *Last Voyage of John Ross*, p. 18.

Isaac de la Peyrère, *Relation du Groenland* (The Hague, 1693), quoted in Crantz, *History of Greenland*, vol. 1, bk. 4, p. 277.

William Baffin, "The Fourth Voyage of James Hall to Groenland . . . 1612," in Clements R. Markham, ed., *The Voyages of William Baffin*, Hakluyt Society Series 1, vol. 63 (London, 1881), p. 24.

PAGE SIXTEEN

George Beste, "A True Discourse of the Late Voyages of Discoverie . . . Under the Conduct of Martin Frobisher, General" (London, 1578), in Rear-Admiral Richard Collinson, ed., *The Three Voyages of Martin Frobisher in Search of a Passage to Cathaia and India by the North-West A.D. 1576–1578*, Hakluyt Society Series 1, vol. 38 (London, 1867), p. 134.

William Scoresby, Jr., *An Account of the Arctic Regions with a History and Description of the Northern Whale-Fishery* (Edinburgh, 1820), vol. 1, pp. 491–96, quoted in F. E. Beddard, *A Book of Whales* (London: John Murray, 1900), p. 248.

Peyrère, quoted in Crantz, *History of Greenland*, vol. 1, bk. 4, p. 278.

Edward Topsell, *The History of Four-footed Beasts and Serpents, and Insects* (New York: Da Capo Press, 1967 [facsimile of London edition of 1658]), vol. 1, pp. 554–55.

Huish, *Last Voyage of John Ross*, p. 170.

John Gatonbe, "A Voyage into the North-West Passage, Undertaken in the Year 1612," from Awnsham Churchill and John Churchill, comps., *A Collection of Voyages and Travels . . .* (London: J. Walthoe, 1732), vol. 5, reprinted in Markham, ed., *Voyages of Baffin*, p. 13.

Caption: Peyrère, *Relation du Groenland*, in Adam White, ed., *A Collection of Documents on Spitzbergen and Greenland*, Hakluyt Society Series 1, vol. 18 (London, 1855), p. 199.

PAGE EIGHTEEN

All quotations from John Ross, *A Voyage of Discovery Made Under Orders of the Admiralty in His Majesty's Ships Isabella and Alexander, for the Purpose of Exploring Baffin's Bay . . .* (London: John Murray, 1819), pp. 80–89.

PAGE TWENTY

Epigraph: Baffin, "Fourth Voyage," in Markham, ed., *Voyages of Baffin*, p. 37.

William Thalbitzer, "Ethnographical Collections from East Greenland made by G. Holm, G. Amdrup, and J. Peterson," *Meddelelser om Grønland* 39 (1914): 486, footnote.

See Charles Francis Hall, *Arctic Researches and Life Among the Esquimaux . . . in the Years 1860, 1861, 1862* (New York: Harper & Brothers, 1865).

Ross, *Voyage of Discovery*, p. 104.

Robert E. Peary, *Northward Over the "Great Ice," a Narrative of Work . . . Upon the Interior Ice Cap of Northern Greenland in the Years 1886 and 1891–97* (New York: Frederick A. Stokes Co., 1898), vol. 2, p. 145.

PAGE TWENTY-TWO

All quotations from Thomas Ellis, *A True Report of the Third and Last Voyage into Meta Incognita: Atchieved by the Worthie Capteine M. Martine Frobisher Esquire, Anno 1578* (London: Thomas Dawson, 1578).

PAGE TWENTY-FOUR

Epigraph: Alexander Armstrong, *A Personal Narrative of the Discovery of the North-West Passage; with Numerous Incidents of Travel . . .* (London: Hurst & Blackett, 1857), p. 145.

PAGE TWENTY-SIX

Beste, "A True Discourse," in Collinson, *Voyages of Frobisher*, pp. 141–42.

Peary, *Northward*, vol. 1, p. 203.

Josephine Diebitsch Peary, *My Arctic Journal: A Year Among Ice-fields and Eskimos* (London: Longmans, Green & Co., 1894), pp. 125–26.

Caption: Lyon, *Private Journal*, p. 72.

PAGE TWENTY-EIGHT

Epigraph: Editorial, *New York Times*, July 24, 1873.

Adolphus W. Greely, Diary, October 9, 1883, in *Three Years of Arctic Service, an Account of the Lady Franklin Bay Expedition of 1881–84 . . .* (New York: Charles Scribner's Sons, 1886), vol. 2, p. 162.

Private Roderick Schneider, Diary, June 1884, quoted in Greely, *Three Years*, vol. 2, p. 321.

Greely, Diary, June 9, 1884, in *Three Years*, vol. 2, p. 323.

Adolphus W. Greely, Order for Private Henry's Execution, June 6th, 1884, in U.S. House of Representatives, *Report on the Proceedings of the United States Expedition to Lady Franklin Bay, Grinnell Land*, 49th cong., 1st sess., H. R. Miscellaneous Documents no. 393 (Washington: Government Printing Office, 1888), p. 363.

Lieutenant David L. Brainard, Field Journal, April 6, 1882, quoted in Greely, *Three Years*, vol. 1, p. 299.

Private Julius Frederick, Report of the Death of Sergeant Rice, U.S. War Department, n.d., quoted in Bessie Rowland James, ed., *Six Came Back: The Arctic Adventure of David L. Brainard* (Indianapolis: Bobbs-Merrill Co., 1940), p. 261.

PAGE THIRTY

Epigraph: Admiral Robert E. Peary, *The North Pole: Its Discovery in 1909 Under the Auspices of the Peary Arctic Club* (New York: Frederick A. Stokes Co., 1910), p. 41.

Ibid., p. 26

Ibid., p. 15

PAGE THIRTY-TWO

Epigraph: Ibid., pp. 9–10.

PAGE THIRTY-FOUR

Epigraph: Ibid., p. 281.

Ibid., p. 229.

R. Peary, *Nearest the Pole*, p. 145.

R. Peary, *The North Pole*, p. 281.

PAGE THIRTY-SIX

Epigraph: Knud Rasmussen, "The Seal Eskimos: Simplicity Through Poverty," in Carleton S. Coon, *A Reader in General Anthropology* (New York: Holt, Rinehart & Winston, 1964), p. 119.

R. Peary, *The North Pole*, p. 271.

New York Times, October 3, 1926, p. 6.

PAGE THIRTY-EIGHT

Epigraph: Herman Melville, *Moby-Dick; or, The Whale* (Indianapolis: Bobbs-Merrill Co., 1964), chap. 42.

R. Peary, *Nearest the Pole*, p. 51.

Robert E. Peary, "The Great White Journey From McCormick Bay to the Northern Shore of Greenland and Return," in J. Peary, *Arctic Journal*, p. 232.

R. Peary, *The North Pole*, p. 199.

Ibid., p. 298.

Ibid., p. 7.

Caption: Ibid., p. 195.

PAGE FORTY

Epigraph: *New York Times*, September 5, 1909, p. 1.

New York Times, September 7, 1909, p. 1.

Dr. Ellis Stroemgren, president of the examining committee, quoted in the *New York Times*, December 22, 1909, p. 2.

PAGE FORTY-TWO

Epigraph: Lieutenant Fitzhugh Green, "Arctic Duty with the Crocker Land Expedition," *Proceedings of the United States Naval Institute* 43, no. 175 (September 1917): 1948.

Robert E. Peary, quoted in ibid., p. 1947.

New York Times, September 5, 1909, p. 1.

Green, "Arctic Duty," p. 1947.

Matthew A. Henson, *A Negro Explorer at the North Pole* (New York: Frederick A. Stokes Co., 1912), p. 188.

Green, "Arctic Duty," p. 1948.

Commander Robert E. Peary, "The Value of Arctic Exploration," *National Geographic Magazine* 14 (December 1903): 443.

Caption: Beste, "A True Discourse," in Collinson, ed., *Voyages of Frobisher*, p. 73.

THE CONGO

PAGE FORTY-EIGHT

Epigraph: Lang to a friend, n.d., quoted in Mary Cynthia Dickerson, "In the Heart of Africa," *American Museum Journal* (American Museum of Natural History, New York) 10, no. 6 (October 1910): 147.

Henry Morton Stanley, *In Darkest Africa, or the Quest, Rescue, and Retreat of Emin, Governor of Equatoria* (New York: Charles Scribner's Sons, 1890), vol. 2, p. 76.

James P. Chapin, Unpublished Reminiscences, r.2b, p. 5, Ornithology Department Archives, American Museum of Natural History, New York.

PAGE FIFTY

Epigraph: Aristotle, *Historia Animalium* 606^{b}20.

Chapin, Unpublished Reminiscences, r.4a, p. 5.

Chapin to Dr. Streeter of the Explorers Club, December 29, 1957, p. 4, Ornithology Department Archives, American Museum of Natural History, New York.

Chapin, Unpublished Reminiscences, V a, p. 1.

Chapin, *New York Herald*, March 30, 1915, p. 6.

James P. Chapin, Congo Expedition Diaries, February 2–4, 1910, Ornithology Department Archives, American Museum of Natural History, New York.

Herbert Lang and James P. Chapin, "Nesting Habits of the African Hornbill," *American Museum Journal* 18, no. 4 (April 1918): 271–74.

Caption: Herbert Lang, Congo Expedition Field Notes, February 6, 1910, Mammalogy Department Archives, American Museum of Natural History, New York. Herbert Lang, "Nomad Dwarfs and Civilization," *Natural History* (American Museum of Natural History, New York) 19, no. 6 (December 1919): 710.

PAGE FIFTY-TWO

Epigraph: Joseph Conrad, *Heart of Darkness* (Harmondsworth, Eng.: Penguin Books, 1973), p. 48.

Stanley, *In Darkest Africa*, vol. 2, p. 76.

Ibid., p. 76.

Herbert Lang and James P. Chapin, "Bats of the Belgian Congo," *American Museum Journal* 17, no. 8 (December 1916): 560–61.

Stanley, *In Darkest Africa*, p. 93.

Patrick Putnam, "The Pygmies of the Ituri Forest," in Coon, *Reader in General Anthropology*, p. 340.

Ibid., p. 341.

Caption: J. A. Allen, Herbert Lang, and James P. Chapin, "The American Museum Congo Expedition Collection of Bats," *Bulletin of the American Museum of Natural History* 38 (September 29, 1917): 480–81.

PAGE FIFTY-FOUR

Epigraph: "The Second Voyage of Sinbad," *The Thousand and One Nights, commonly called in England, The Arabian Nights' Entertainments*, trans. Edward William Lane (London: Chas. Knight & Co., 1839–41), vol. 3, p. 18. "The Fifth Voyage of Sinbad," *A Plain and Literal Translation of the Arabian Nights' Entertainments . . .* trans. Richard F. Burton (privately printed, n.d.), vol. 6, p. 49.

All quotations from James P. Chapin, "The Crowned Eagle, Ogre of Africa's Monkeys," *Natural History* 25, no. 5 (September–October 1925): 459–69.

Caption: Paul Du Chaillu, ca. 1855, in James P. Chapin, Unpublished Papers, 1925–1934, Ornithology Department Archives, American Museum of Natural History, New York.

PAGE FIFTY-SIX

Epigraph: Conrad, *Heart of Darkness*, p. 29.

R. Meinertzhagen to Chapin, July 30, 1944, Ornithology Department Archives, American Museum of Natural History, New York.

Chapin, Unpublished Papers, n.d., n.p.

Emory Ross (missionary), private communication to Chapin, February 25, 1941, Ornithology Department Archives, American Museum of Natural History, New York.

Harry Raven (mammalogist), private communication to Chapin, April 15, 1942, Ornithology Department Archives, American Museum of Natural History, New York.

Caption: Chapin, Unpublished Papers, n.d., n.p.. Reverend William Holman Bentley, *Pioneering on the Congo* (London: Religious Tract Society, 1900), vol. 2. p. 245.

PAGE FIFTY-EIGHT

Epigraph: Colin M. Turnbull, *The Forest People* (New York: Simon & Schuster, 1962), pp. 92–93.

James Henry Breasted, *Ancient Records of Egypt: Historical Documents from the Earliest Times to the Persian Conquest* (Chicago: University of Chicago Press, 1906–7), vol. 1, p. 161, par. 353.

Olfert Dapper, *Umbstandliche und Eigentliche Beschreifung von Afrika* (1670), quoted in Paul Schebesta, *Among Congo Pigmies*, trans. Gerald Griffin (London: Hutchinson & Co., 1933).

Turnbull, *The Forest People*, p. 260.

Caption: Chapin, quoted in John K. Terres, "On the Trail of Congo Jim," *Audubon Magazine* (National Audubon Society, New York) 48, no. 4 (July–August 1946): 235.

PAGE SIXTY

Epigraph: David Livingstone, *Missionary Travels and Researches in South Africa*, 25th ed. (New York: Harper & Brothers, 1859), p. 651.

Putnam, "Pygmies of the Ituri," p. 330.

Jean Janmart, "Elephant Hunting as Practiced by the Congo Pygmies," *American Anthropologist* (American Anthropological Association, Menasha, Wis.) 54, no. 1 (January–March 1952) 146–47.

Putnam, "Pygmies of the Ituri," pp. 330–33.

PAGE SIXTY-TWO

Epigraphs: Tiglath-pileser I (ca. 1100 B.C.), inscription from Kalat Sherkat on the east bank of the Tigris (now in the British Museum), quoted in George F. Kunz, *Ivory and the Elephant in Art, in Archaeology, and in Science* (Garden City, N.Y.: Doubleday, Page, & Co., 1916), p. 192. Pliny the Elder, *Natural History* (ca. 55 A.D.), trans. H. Rackham (Cambridge, Mass.: Harvard University Press, 1967), 5. 1. 15. Oracle bone fragment, An-yang, China (ca. 1400 B.C.), Hung-hsiang Chou, decipherer, personal communication.

See Pliny, *Natural History* 4.

Caption: Henry Fairfield Osborn, *Proboscidea, a Monograph of the Discovery, Evolution, Migration, and Extinction of the Mastodons and Elephants of the World* (New York: American Museum Press, 1936), vol. 2, p. 1202. Kunz, *Ivory and the Elephant*, p. 411.

PAGE SIXTY-FOUR

Epigraph: Luis de Camoēs, *The Lusiads* 5.13 (1572), quoted in Duarte Lopes, *A Report of the Kingdom of Congo*, ed. Filippo Pigafetta (Rome, 1591), trans. and ed. Margarite Hutchinson (1881; reprint ed., New York: Negro Universities Press, 1969), title page.

See Lopes, *Kingdom of Congo*, throughout.

See also Leo Africanus, *The History and Description of Africa and of the Notable Things Therein Contained* (1526), trans. John Pory (1600), ed. Robert Brown, Hakluyt Society Series 1, vols. 92, 93, 94 (London, 1896).

Caption: Norman Grubb, *Christ in Congo Forests: The Story of The Heart of Africa Mission* (London: Lutterworth Press, 1945), p. 42.

PAGE SIXTY-SIX

Epigraph: James Kingston Tuckey, *Narrative of an Expedition to Explore the River Zaire, Usually Called the Congo, in South Africa, in 1816* (London: John Murray, 1818), pp. 98–99.

Belgian Congo (Brussels: Belgian Congo and Ruanda-Urundi Information and Public Relations Office, 1959), vol. 1, p. 79.

PAGE SIXTY-EIGHT

Epigraph: John Tressart, secretary to King Henry VI of England, quoted in Jules Quicherat, *Procès de Condamnation et de Réhabilitation de Jeanne D'Arc dite la Pucelle* (Paris: Renouard, 1847), vol. 3, p. 182.

Père Laurent de Lucques, "Dixième relation," January 3, 1707, in *Relations sur Le Congo du Père Laurent de Lucques (1700–1717)*, trans. and ed. Mgr. Jean Cuvelier, Institut Royal Colonial Belge, Section des Sciences Morales et Politiques, *Mémoires*, série historique, vol. 32, fasc. 2 (Brussels, 1953), pp. 222–38.

Caption: Chapin, Unpublished Reminiscences, r.2b, p. 2.

PAGE SEVENTY

Epigraph: Professor Christian Smith, Journal, in Tuckey, *Narrative of an Expedition*, p. 331.

Leo Africanus, *History and Description of Africa*, p. 13.

Henry Morton Stanley, *Through the Dark Continent, or the Sources of the Nile, Around the Great Lakes of Equatorial Africa, and Down the Livingstone River to the Atlantic Ocean* (New York: Harper & Brothers, 1879), vol. 2, p. 336.

Tuckey, *Narrative of an Expedition*, editor's introduction, p. xxxiii.

Assistant Surgeon Mr. McKerrow, Report, quoted in ibid., p. xliii.

PAGE SEVENTY-TWO

Epigraph: Stanley, *Through the Dark Continent*, vol. 2, p. 152.

Ibid., p. 99.

Ibid., p. 200.

E. J. Glave, *Six Years of Adventure in Congo-Land* (London: Sampson, Low, Marston & Co., 1893), p. 1.

PAGE SEVENTY-FOUR

Epigraph: Ibid., p. 1.

Various passages: Stanley, *Through the Dark Continent*, vol. 2, pp. 269, 272.

Henry Morton Stanley, *The Exploration Diaries of H. M. Stanley*, ed. Richard Stanley and Alan Neame (London: William Kimber & Co., 1961), pp. 149, 159 (entry for February 2, 1877).

Caption: Chapin, Congo Expedition Diaries, August 15, 1909.

PAGE SEVENTY-SIX

Epigraph: Stanley, *Through the Dark Continent*, vol. 2, p. 312.

Ibid., p. 277.

Stanley, *Exploration Diaries*, p. 160 (entry for February 4, 1877).

Stanley, *Through the Dark Continent*, vol. 2, pp. 305, 309.

Ibid., p. 315.

Ibid., p. 286.

Ibid., p. 283.

PAGE SEVENTY-EIGHT

Epigraph: Stanley, *Exploration Diaries*, p. 193 (entry for June 5, 1877).

All quotations from ibid., pp. 174–77 (entry for March 29, 1877).

PAGE EIGHTY

Epigraph: Chapin to mother and sister, December 27, 1913, p. 2, Ornithology Department Archives, American Museum of Natural History, New York.

All quotations from David Livingstone, *The Last Journals of David Livingstone from 1865 to His Death*, ed. Horace Waller (London: John Murray, 1874), vol. 2, pp. 206–8 (entry for July 7, 1872).

Caption: Georg Schweinfurth, *The Heart of Africa: Three Years' Travels and Adventures in the Unexplored Regions of Central Africa from 1868 to 1871*, trans. Ellen E. Frewer (New York: Harper & Brothers, 1874), vol. 2, p. 79.

PAGE EIGHTY-TWO

Epigraph: Bentley, *Pioneering on the Congo*, vol. 2, p. 210.

Caption: Schebesta, *Among Congo Pigmies*, p. 173.

See also T. Alexander Barnes, *The Wonderland of the Eastern Congo* (New York: G. P. Putnam's Sons, 1922), p. 207.

PAGE EIGHTY-FOUR

James P. Chapin, "Profiteers of the Busy Bee," *Natural History* 24, no. 3 (May–June 1924): 329.

Chapin, Unpublished Reminiscences, p. 22.

Chapin, quoted in John K. Terres, ed., *Discovery: Great Moments in the Lives of Outstanding Naturalists* (Philadelphia: J. B. Lippincott Co., 1961), p. 17.

Chapin, "Profiteers," p. 335.

Chapin, Unpublished Reminiscences, r.4a.

Ibid., pp. 34–37.

Chapin, quoted in Terres, *Discovery*, p. 20.

Chapin, Unpublished Reminiscences, pp. 37–38.

Chapin, quoted in Terres, *Discovery*, p. 24.

PAGE EIGHTY-SIX

Epigraph: Chapin, quoted in Herbert Friedman, "In Memoriam: James Paul Chapin," *The Auk; a Quarterly Journal of Ornithology* (American Ornithologists' Union, Cambridge, Mass.) 83 (April 1966): 245.

Chapin to Dr. Streeter, December 9, 1957, p. 3.

Herbert Lang, "Narrative of the Expedition," in Henry Fairfield Osborn, "The Congo Expedition of the American Museum of Natural History," *Bulletin of the American Museum of Natural History* 34 (August 1, 1919): xxiii.

THE GOBI

PAGE NINETY-TWO

Epigraph: Friar William of Rubruck, *The Journey of William of Rubruck to the Eastern Parts of the World, 1253–1255*, ed. and trans. William Woodville Rockhill, Hakluyt Society Series 2, vol. 4 (London, 1900), p. 133.

Caption: Charles P. Berkey and Frederick K. Morris, *Geology of Mongolia*, in *The Natural History of Central Asia*, ed. Chester A. Reeds (New York: American Museum of Natural History, 1927), vol. 2, p. 194.

PAGE NINETY-FOUR

Epigraphs: John of Plano Carpini, "History of the Mongols" (ca. 1247), in Christopher Dawson, ed., *The Mongol Mission: Narratives and Letters of the Franciscan Missionaries in Mongolia and China in the 13th and 14th Centuries* (New York: Sheed & Ward, 1955), p. 6. Roy Chapman Andrews, Field Journals of the Third Asiatic Expedition, American Museum of Natural History Library, New York, vol. 1, 1922, p. 163.

Roy Chapman Andrews, *The New Conquest of Central Asia: A Narrative of the Explorations of the Central Asiatic Expeditions in Mongolia and China, 1921–1930*, in *The Natural History of Central Asia*, ed. Chester A. Reeds (New York: American Museum of Natural History, 1932), vol. 1, p. 397.

Marco Polo, *The Travels of Marco Polo, a Venetian, in the Thirteenth Century: Being a Description . . . of Remarkable Places and Things, in the Eastern Parts of the World*, trans. William Marsden (London: Cox Baylis, printer; sold by Longman, Hurst, Rees, Orme, & Brown, 1818), p. 158.

Marco Polo, *The Book of Ser Marco Polo, Concerning the Kingdoms and Marvels of the East*, trans. Sir Henry Yule, 3rd ed., rev. Henri Cordier (London, 1926), vol. 1, p. 180.

Fa-hsien, *The Travels of Fa-hsien (399–414 A.D.), or Record of the Buddhistic Kingdoms*, ed. and trans. H. A. Giles (Cambridge: University Press, 1923), p. 2.

Caption: Andrews, *New Conquest*, p. 177.

PAGE NINETY-SIX

Epigraph: Roy Chapman Andrews, *Ends of the Earth* (New York: G. P. Putnam's Sons, 1929), p. 268.

Andrews, *New Conquest*, p. 7.

Andrews, *Ends of the Earth*, p. 249.

W. D. (William Diller) Matthew, Field Files, April 1923, Department of Vertebrate Paleontology Archives, American Museum of National History, New York.

George Gaylord Simpson, "Memorial to Walter Granger" (1941), p. 7, Department of Vertebrate Paleontology Archives, American Museum of Natural History, New York.

Andrews, *New Conquest*, p. 90.

Ibid., p. 39.

Caption: Berkey and Morris, *Geology of Mongolia*, p. 396. Andrews, *New Conquest*, p. 103.

PAGE NINETY-EIGHT

Roy Chapman Andrews, "Explorations in the Gobi Desert," *National Geographic Magazine* 63 (June 1933): 617.

Andrews, *New Conquest*, p. 271.

Ibid., p. 190.

Ibid., p. 197.

Caption: Ibid., pp. 170–71.

PAGE ONE HUNDRED

Roy Chapman Andrews, *On the Trail of Ancient Man* (New York: G. P. Putnam's Sons, 1926), p. 324. Andrews, Field Journals, vol. 1, 1922, pp. 20–21. Andrews, *New Conquest*, pp. 200–1, 360.

PAGE ONE HUNDRED TWO

Epigraph: Ala-ad-Din Ata Malik Juvaini, *The History of the World Conqueror*, trans. John Andrew Boyle (Manchester: Manchester University Press, 1958), vol. 1, p. 27.

Walter Granger, "Camp Life in the Gobi Desert," *Natural History* 31 (July–August 1931): 336.

Juvaini, *World Conqueror*, vol. 1, pp. 28–29.

PAGE ONE HUNDRED FOUR

Epigraph: Andrews, *New Conquest*, p. 380.

All quotations from Sven Hedin, *Through Asia* (New York: Harper & Brothers, 1899), vol. 1, pp. 562–84.

PAGE ONE HUNDRED SIX

Epigraph: Eduard Evan Evans-Pritchard, *The Nuer: A Description of the Modes of Livelihood and Political Institutions of a Nilotic People* (Oxford: Clarendon Press, 1940), p. 26.

General Ma Yüan (14 B.C.–A.D. 49), quoted in Herrlee G. Creel, "The Role of the Horse in Chinese History," *American Historical Review* (American Historical Association, Washington, D.C.) 70, no. 3 (October 1964–July 1965): 659. See also Sergei I. Rudenko, *Frozen Tombs of Siberia: The Pazyryk Burials of Iron Age Horsemen*, trans. M. W. Thompson (Berkeley: University of California Press, 1970), pp. xxv–xxvi. W. Perceval Yetts, "The Horse: A Factor in Early Chinese History," *Eurasia Septentrionalis Antigua*, vol. 9 (Minns Volume), Helsinki, 1934. James F. Downs, "The Origin and Spread of Riding in the Near East and Central Asia," *American Anthropologist* 63, no. 6 (December 1961): 1193–1201. Friedrich Hirth, "The Story of Chang K'ien, China's Pioneer in Western Asia," *Journal of the American Oriental Society* (Yale University Press for the Society) 37 (1917): 107–12.

Caption: Ssu-Ma Ch'ien, *Shih chi*, quoted in Friedrich Hirth, *The Ancient History of China to the End of the Chou Dynasty* (New York: Columbia University Press, 1911), p. 168. Andrews, *New Conquest*, p. 128. Ibid., p. 21.

PAGE ONE HUNDRED EIGHT

Epigraph: Voltaire, "Essai sur l'Histoire Général," vol. 3, chap. 60, in *The Works of M. de Voltaire*, trans. and ed. T. Smollet and T. Francklin (London: J. Newbery, 1762), vol. 2, p. 143.

Andrews, *New Conquest*, p. 413.

Sir Gerard Clauson, *Turkish and Mongolian Studies* (London: Royal Asiatic Society of Great Britain and Ireland, 1962), p. 15.

Ibid., p. 9.

Francis Woodman Cleaves, trans., *The Secret History of the Mongols, For the First Time Done into English out of the Original Tongue and Provided with an Exegetical Commentary* (Cambridge, Mass.: Harvard University Press, forthcoming), p. 1.

PAGE ONE HUNDRED TEN

Epigraph: Charles Bawden, trans. and notes, "The Mongol Chronicle Altan Tobči," *Göttinger Asiatische Forschungen* (Wiesbaden: Otto Harrassowitz, 1955), vol. 5, p. 134.

Cleaves, *Secret History*, p. 14.

Ibid., p. 191.

Ibid., p. 26.

H. Desmond Martin, *The Rise of Chingis Khan and His Conquest of North China*

(Baltimore: Johns Hopkins University Press, 1950), p. 228.

J. J. Saunders, *The History of the Mongol Conquests* (London: Routledge & Kegan Paul, 1971), p. 63.

Meng Hung and Juvaini, quoted in W. Barthold, *Turkestan Down to the Mongol Invasion*, 2nd ed., trans. and rev. by author with assistance of H. A. R. Gibb (London: Luzac & Co., 1958).

Caption: Andrews, Field Journals, vol. 1, 1922, p. 45.

PAGE ONE HUNDRED TWELVE

Epigraph: Father Joseph de Mailla, *Histoire générale de la Chine* (Paris, 1777–83), in Martin, *Rise of Chingis Khan*, p. 297.

Grigor of Akanc', "History of the Nation of Archers (the Mongols)," ed. and trans. Robert P. Blake and Richard N. Frye, *Harvard Journal of Asiatic Studies* (Harvard-Yenching Institute, Cambridge, Mass.) 12, nos. 3, 4 (December 1949): 305.

Bawden, "Altan Tobči," p. 132.

Martin, *Rise of Chingis Khan*, pp. 205, 178.

Juvaini, quoted in Barthold, *Turkestan*, p. 394.

Juvaini, *World Conqueror*, vol. 1. p. 177.

The Chronicle of Novgorod, 1016–1471, trans. Robert Mitchell and Nevill Forbes, Royal Historical Society (Camden Society) Publications, Series 3, vol. 25 (London, 1914), p. 81.

Great Khan Guyuk to Pope Innocent IV, A.D. 1246, Vatican Archive, trans. William Boyle, quoted in Igor de Rachewiltz, "The Hsi-Yu Lu by Yeh-Lu Ch'u Ts'ai," *Monumenta Serica, Journal of Oriental Studies of the Catholic University* (Henri Vetch, Peking) 21 (1962): 213.

Great Khan Guyuk, quoted by Dawson, *The Mongol Mission*, p. 83.

Caption: Roy Chapman Andrews, *Across Mongolian Plains* (New York: D. Appleton & Co., 1921), p. 81.

PAGE ONE HUNDRED FOURTEEN

Epigraph: *Chronicle of Novgorod*, pp. 81, 65.

Martin, *Rise of Chingis Khan*, p. 19.

Harold T. Cheshire, "The Great Tartar Invasion of Europe," *Slavonic Review* (School of Slavonic Studies, University of London) 5 (1926–27): 90.

Juvaini, *World Conqueror*, vol. 1, p. 30.

Marsden, trans., *Travels of Marco Polo*, vol. 1, chap. 48.

Captain B. H. Liddell Hart, "Mongol Campaigns," *Encyclopædia Britannica*, 1956, vol. 15, p. 708.

Juvaini, *World Conqueror*, vol. 1, p., 30.

Hulagu Khan to the Mamelukes of Egypt, ca. A.D. 1261, quoted in Sir Henry Howorth, *History of the Mongols from the 9th to the 19th Century* (London: Longmans, Green & Co., 1880–1927), pt. 3, pp. 165–66.

PAGE ONE HUNDRED SIXTEEN

Epigraph: Sumerian inscription from Ur in Mesopotamia, ca. 1950 B.C. (Third Dynasty), in Grahame Clark and Stuart Piggott, *Prehistoric Societies* (New York: Alfred A. Knopf, 1965), p. 284.

William of Rubruck, *Journey*, p. 220.

Ibid., p. 254.

Ibid., p. 140.

Edward Gibbon, *The History of the Decline and Fall of the Roman Empire* (Philadelphia: William Birch & Abraham Small, 1804), vol. 4, p. 243.

Martin, *Rise of Chingis Khan*, p. 296, quoting Jean-Pierre-Abel Rémusat, "Vie de Yeliu Thsoutsai," *Nouveaux Mélanges Asiatiques* (Paris, 1829), vol. 2.

Jorge Luis Borges, "Story of the Warrior and the Captive," *A Personal Anthology*, trans. and ed. Anthony Kerrigan (New York: Grove Press, 1967), p. 172.

PAGE ONE HUNDRED EIGHTEEN

Epigraph: Chinggis Khan, *Bilik* [Codes], quoted in Martin, *Rise of Chingis Khan*, p. 315.

Yule, trans., *Ser Marco Polo*, vol. 2, p. 355.

Marsden, trans., *Travels of Marco Polo*, vol. 1, pp. 251–52.

Howorth, *Mongols*, pt. 1, p. 240.

Bawden, "Altan Tobči," p. 153.

Yule, trans., *Ser Marco Polo*, vol. 1, p. 268, citing Évariste Régis Huc.

PAGE ONE HUNDRED TWENTY

Epigraph: From *Haft Iklím* [The Seven Climates], a Persian geography, quoted by Yule in *Ser Marco Polo*, vol. 1, p. 179, footnote.

Owen Lattimore, "A Ruined Nestorian City in Inner Mongolia," in *Studies in Frontier History: Collected Papers, 1928–1958* (London: Oxford University Press, 1962), pp. 221–23.

Ibid., pp. 229, 230.

Owen Lattimore, *Mongol Journeys* (New York: Doubleday, Doran & Co., 1941), pp. 106–7.

William of Rubruck, *Journey*, p. 182.

See Desmond Martin, "Preliminary Report on Nestorian Remains North of Keui-Hua, Suiyüan," *Monumenta Serica* 3 (1938): 232–42.

Lattimore, *Mongol Journeys*, p. 109.

PAGE ONE HUNDRED TWENTY-TWO

All quotations from Andrews, *New Conquest*, pp. 208–10.

Caption: Ibid., p. 257.

PAGE ONE HUNDRED TWENTY-FOUR

Epigraph: Charles Darwin, *A Naturalist's Voyage, Journal of Researches into the Natural History and Geology of the Countries Visited during the Voyage of H.M.S. 'Beagle' Round the World*, 2nd ed. (London: John Murray, 1889), pp. 146–47.

Caption: Andrews, *New Conquest*, p. 130. Andrews, *Ends of the Earth*, p. 226.

PAGE ONE HUNDRED TWENTY-SIX

Epigraph: W. H. Hudson, *The Naturalist in La Plata* (1892), quoted in W. H. Edwards, *The Early History of Paleontology* (London: Trustees of the British Museum, 1967), p. 223.

All quotations from Andrews, *New Conquest*, pp. 434–35, 406, 444.

PAGE ONE HUNDRED TWENTY-EIGHT

Epigraph: M. [Évariste Régis] Huc, *Recollections of a Journey through Tartary, Thibet, and China, during the years 1844, 1845, 1846* (New York: D. Appleton & Co., 1852), vol. 1, p. 25.

Andrews, "Explorations in the Gobi Desert," p. 655.

Andrews, *New Conquest*, p. 89.

Ibid., p. 346.

Ibid., p. 57.

Caption: Ibid., p. 184. Also Lieutenant Colonel N. Prejevalsky, *Mongolia, the Tangut Country, and the Solitudes of Northern Tibet*, trans. Delmar Morgan (London: Sampson Low, Marston, Low & Searle, 1876), p. 56.

PAGE ONE HUNDRED THIRTY

Epigraph: Gibbon, *Decline and Fall*, vol. 8, p. 27.

Pliny, *Natural History* 6. 20. 54.

Huc, *Recollections*, vol. 1, p. 65.

Andrews, *Across Mongolian Plains*, pp. 6–7.

Caption: Lattimore, *Mongol Journeys*, p. 150.

SIBERIA

PAGE ONE HUNDRED THIRTY-SIX

Epigraph: Father Joseph de Acosta, *The Natural and Moral History of the Indies*, trans. Edward Grimstone (1604), ed. Clements R. Markham, Hakluyt Society Series 1, vol. 60 (London, 1880), p. 60.

PAGE ONE HUNDRED THIRTY-EIGHT

Epigraph: Boas to Jochelson, n.d., Anthropology Department Archives, American Museum of Natural History, New York.

Jochelson to Boas, July 4, 1902, p. 7, Anthropology Department Archives, American Museum of Natural History.

PAGE ONE HUNDRED FORTY

Epigraph: Herodotus, *Histories* 4. 26.

Waldemar Jochelson, "The Koryak," *American Museum of Natural History Memoir*, vol. 10 (New York, 1905), pt. 2, p. 396.

Ferdinand von Wrangell, *Narrative of an Expedition to the Polar Sea in the Years 1820, 1821, & 1823 . . .*, ed. Lieutenant-Colonel Edward Sabine, 2nd ed. (London: James Madden, 1884), pp. 48, 373.

PAGE ONE HUNDRED FORTY-TWO

Epigraph: Gilyak girl from southern Sakhalin Island quoted by Berthold Laufer in Franz Boas, "The Jesup North Pacific Expedition," *American Museum Journal* 3, no. 5 (October 1903): 97.

Bogoras to Boas, July 25–26, 1900, Boas Correspondence, American Philosophical Society, Philadelphia, Pa.

Jochelson, "The Koryak," pt. 2, pp. 430, 427.

Ibid., p. 427.

Jochelson to Boas, December 3, 1900, p. 9, Anthropology Department Archives, American Museum of Natural History, New York.

Caption: George Kennan, *Tent Life in Siberia . . . Adventures among the Koryaks and other Tribes in Kamchatka and Northern Asia* (New York: G. P. Putnam's Sons, 1910), p. 168.

PAGE ONE HUNDRED FORTY-FOUR

Epigraph: Adelbert von Chamisso, "Remarks and Opinions of the Naturalist," in Otto von Kotzebue, *A Voyage of Discovery into the South Sea and Beering's Straits . . . undertaken in the years 1815–1818*, trans. H. E. Lloyd (London: Longman, Hurst, 1821), vol. 3, p. 261.

See A. P. Okladnikov, *The Ancient Population of Siberia and Its Cultures*, trans. Vladimir M. Maurin, Peabody Museum of Archaeology and Ethnology, Harvard University, Russian Translation Series, no. 1 (Cambridge, Mass., 1959).

A. P. Okladnikov, *Yakutia Before Its Incorporation into the Russian State*, ed. Henry N. Michael, Arctic Institute of North America, Anthropology of the North Series, Translations from Russian Sources, no. 8 (Montreal: McGill-Queen's University Press, 1970).

S. I. Rudenko, *The Ancient Culture of the Bering Sea and the Eskimo Problem*, trans. Paul Tolstoy, Arctic Institute of North America, Anthropology of the North Series, Translations from Russian Sources, no. 1 (Toronto: University of Toronto Press, 1961).

PAGE ONE HUNDRED FORTY-SIX

Epigraph: Okladnikov, *Ancient Population of Siberia*, p. 33, cites this as "traditional."

Waldemar Jochelson, "The Yukaghir and Yukaghirized Tungus," *American Museum of Natural History Memoir*, vol. 9, pt. 1 (New York, 1910), p. 20.

Martin Sauer, *An Account of a Geographical and Astronomical Expedition to the Northern Parts of Russia performed by Commodore Joseph Billings in the years 1785 to 1794* (London: T. Cadell & W. Davies, 1802), p. 61.

Waldemar Bogoras, "The Chukchee," *American Museum of Natural History Memoir*, vol. 11, pt. 1 (New York, 1904), p. 133.

Caption: Waldemar Bogoras, "Culture of the Circumpolar Zone," *American Anthropologist* 31, no. 4 (1929): 583.

PAGE ONE HUNDRED FORTY-EIGHT

Epigraph: Lotterus, on a chart published in 1765, in A. E. Nordenskiöld, *The Voyage of the Vega*, trans. Alexander Leslie (London: Macmillan & Co., 1881), vol. 2, p. 77.

Bogoras, "The Chukchee," pt. 3, p. 651.

Ibid., pp. 693–97, 651.

F. A. Golder, *Russian Expansion on the Pacific: An Account of the Earliest and Later Expeditions Made by the Russians along the Pacific Coast of Asia and North America . . .* (1914; reprint ed., Gloucester, Mass.: Peter Smith, n.d.), p. 164.

Bogoras, "The Chukchee," pt. 3, p. 697.

Ibid., pt. 1, p. 15.

PAGE ONE HUNDRED FIFTY

Kennan, *Tent Life in Siberia*, p. 255.

Jochelson, "The Koryak," pt. 2, p. 456.

Kennan, *Tent Life in Siberia*, p. 220.

Caption: Jochelson, "The Koryak," pt. 2, p. 457; pt. 1, pp. 42, 78.

PAGE ONE HUNDRED FIFTY-TWO

Epigraph: Georg Wilhelm Steller, "Journal," trans. Leonhard Stejneger, in F. A. Golder, *Bering's Voyages: An Account of the Efforts of the Russians to Determine the Relation of Asia to America*, American Geographical Society Research Series, no. 1 (New York, 1922, 1925), vol. 2, p. 116.

Vitus Bering, quoted by Steller, "Journal," in Golder, *Bering's Voyages*, vol. 2, p. 34.

Steller, "Journal," in Golder, *Bering's Voyages*, vol. 2, p. 37.

Ibid., p. 116.

Ibid., pp. 137, 146.

Ibid., pp. 183, 186.

Caption: Alexandre von Humboldt, *Fragmens de Géologie*, vol. 2, p. 338, cited in Sir Charles Lyell, *Principles of Geology*, 10th ed., rev. (London: John Murray, 1867), vol. 1, p. 179.

PAGE ONE HUNDRED FIFTY-FOUR

Epigraph: Gerhard Müller, *Voyages from Asia to America for completing the discoveries of the North-West Coast of America*, trans. from the High Dutch (London: Thomas Jefferys, 1761), p. iii.

Simon Dezhnev, "Deshnev's Report," in Golder, *Russian Expansion*, app. B, p. 287.

William Coxe, *Account of the Russian Discoveries between Asia and America. To which is added the Conquest of Siberia . . .*, 4th ed. enlarged (London: Cadell & Davies, 1804), pp. 384–85.

Müller, *Voyages*, p. ix.

Coxe, *Russian Discoveries*, p. 385.

Stepan Petrovich Krasheninnikov, *The History of Kamchatka and the Kurilski Islands, with the Countries Adjacent*, trans. James Grieve, abridged ed. (London: Thomas Jefferys, 1764), p. 240.

PAGE ONE HUNDRED FIFTY-SIX

Epigraph: John Muir, *The Cruise of the Corwin: Journal of the Arctic Expedition of 1881 in Search of De Long and the Jeannette* (Boston: Houghton Mifflin Co., Riverside Press, 1917), pp. 108–9.

Edward W. Nelson, "The Eskimo About Bering Strait," Smithsonian Institution, Bureau of American Ethnology, *18th Annual Report, 1896–1897* (Washington: Government Printing Office, 1899), pt. 1, p. 269.

Captain C. L. Hooper, *Report of the Cruise of the Revenue Steamer Thomas Corwin in the Arctic Ocean, 1881* (Washington: Government Printing Office, 1884), p. 100.

Nelson, "Eskimo About Bering Strait," p. 269.

Hooper, *Cruise of Steamer Corwin*, p. 100.

Bogoras to Boas, September 11, 1901, Boas Correspondence, American Philosophical Society, Philadelphia. Pa.

Caption: Jochelson, "The Koryak," pt. 2, p. 455.

PAGE ONE HUNDRED FIFTY-EIGHT

Epigraph: Chukchee shaman, quoted in Bogoras, "The Chukchee," pt. 2, p. 295.

Waldemar Bogoras, "The Folklore of Northeastern Asia, as Compared with that of Northwestern America," *American Anthropologist* 4, no. 4 (October–December 1902): 582.

Jochelson, "The Koryak," pt. 1, p. 28.

Ibid., p. 97.

PAGE ONE HUNDRED SIXTY

Epigraph: Chukchee shaman, quoted in Bogoras, "Folklore of Northeastern Asia," p. 582.

All quotations from Jochelson, "The Yukaghir," pt. 2, pp. 165–67.

Caption: Jochelson, "The Koryak," pt. 1, pp. 80–81.

PAGE ONE HUNDRED SIXTY-TWO

Epigraph: Lieutenant Yushin Khitrov. "Log Book of the *St. Peter*," in Golder, *Bering's Voyages*, vol. 1, p. 238.

Steller, "Journal," in Golder, *Bering's Voyages*, vol. 2, p. 140.

George William Steller, "The Beasts of the Sea," trans. Walter Miller and Jennie Emerson Miller, in David Starr Jordan and others, *The Fur Seals and Fur-Seal Islands of the Pacific Ocean*, pt. 3 (Washington: Government Printing Office, 1899), pp. 186, 191.

Steller, "Description of Bering Island," in Golder, *Bering's Voyages*, vol. 2, p. 232.

Ibid., p. 227.

Ibid., p. 233.

Sauer, *Geographical Expedition*, p. 181.

PAGE ONE HUNDRED SIXTY-FOUR

Epigraph: El-Mas'udi, *El-Mas'udi's Historical Encyclopedia entitled 'Meadows of Gold and Mines of Gems'* (A.D. 950), trans. Aloys Sprenger (London: Oriental Translation Fund of Great Britain and Ireland, 1841), vol. 1, p. 230.

Pallas to Thomas Pennant, August 13, 1778, in Carol Unress, ed., *A Naturalist in Russia: Letters from Peter Simon Pallas to Thomas Pennant* (Minneapolis: University of Minnesota Press, 1967), p. 32.

See J. L. Davies, "Pleistocene Geography and the Distribution of Northern Pinnipeds," *Ecology* (Ecological Society of America and Duke University Press, Durham, N.C.) 39, no. 1 (January 1958): 104–7.

See S. I. Ognev, *Mammals of the U.S.S.R. and Adjacent Countries*, trans. A. Birron and Z. Cole, Israel Program for Scientific Translations for the National Science Foundation, Washington, D.C. (Jerusalem, 1962), vol. 3, p. 475.

See R. F. Flint and H. G. Dorsey, "Glaciation of Siberia," *Bulletin of the Geological Society of America* (New York) 56 (January 1945): 85.

Bogoras, "The Chukchee," pt. 1, p. 120.

Caption: Ibid., p. 37.

PAGE ONE HUNDRED SIXTY-SIX

Epigraph: Muir, *Cruise of the Corwin*, p. 58.

Wrangell, *Expedition to the Polar Sea*, p. 282.

Bogoras, "The Chukchee," pt. 1, pp. 133–34.

PAGE ONE HUNDRED SIXTY-EIGHT

Epigraph: Catherine II of Russia to Voltaire, October 1771, in Herbert Lang, "Problems and Facts About Frozen Siberian Mammoths (Elephas primigenius), and Their Ivory," *Zoologica; Scientific Contributions of the New York Zoological Society* 4, no. 2 (January 8, 1925): 50.

Lang, "Frozen Siberian Mammoths," pp. 45–47.

Caption: Bogoras, "The Chukchee," pt. 1, p. 201.

PAGE ONE HUNDRED SEVENTY

Epigraph: Jesup to President McKinley, April 13, 1897, in Geoffrey Hellman, *Bankers, Bones, and Beetles: The First Century of the American Museum of Natural History* (Garden City, N.Y.: Natural History Press, 1968), p. 83.

Franz Boas, "The Jesup North Pacific Expedition," *Proceedings of the International Congress of Americanists*, 13th sess. (New York, 1902), p. 99.

PAGE ONE HUNDRED SEVENTY-TWO

Epigraph: Acosta, *Natural and Moral History of the Indies*, vol. 1, p. 45, of 1590 Seville ed., quoted in Ralph L. Beals, "Father Acosta on the First Peopling of the New World," *American Antiquity* (Society for American Archaeology, Menasha, Wis.) 23, no. 2 (1957): 182.

Hooper, *Cruise of Steamer Corwin*, p. 103.

Gawrila Sarytschew (Sarichev), *Account of a Voyage of Discovery to the North-East of Siberia, the Frozen Ocean, and the North-East Sea* (London: Richard Phillips, 1806), vol. 2, p. 49.

Bogoras, "The Chukchee," pt. 3, p. 661.

See Lyell, *Principles of Geology*, vol. 2, p. 448.

Captain Sir Edward Belcher, *Narrative of a Voyage Round the World performed in her Majesty's ship Sulphur During the Years 1836–1842* (London: Henry Coburn, 1843), vol. 1. pp. 304–5.

See also Charles Walcott Brooks, "Japanese Wrecks Stranded and Picked Up Adrift in the North Pacific Ocean," read before the California Academy of Sciences, March 1, 1875, and reprinted from the *Proceedings* of the Academy (San Francisco, 1876).

PAGE ONE HUNDRED SEVENTY-FOUR

Epigraph: Darwin, *A Naturalist's Voyage*, p. 132.

PHOTOGRAPH NEGATIVE NUMBERS

All negatives are in the American Museum of Natural History unless otherwise noted.

ARCTIC CHAPTER	CONGO CHAPTER	GOBI CHAPTER	SIBERIA CHAPTER
33758	112341	411065	11041
98 Janet Lehr Collection	221276	258315	1679/6999
15272	111732	265294	4129/6468
17023	223212	251088	1520/6616
23092	112184	16	4178/6768
23087	226257	252857	11040
123398-A National Geographic Society	111382	410770	1996
17099	221241	241792	4136/6505
232240	111920	251264	11006
122616-A NGS	224621	251193	1783/7233
23355	224244	251195	1423/6359
232682	279829	108699	4139/6508
3851	223980	251353	1562/6677
NP 106 Bowdoin College	227467	97	1450/6437
123286-A NGS	112148, 111783	410746	4169/6726
123269-A NGS	225742	241768	1950
119960-A NGS	111282	241816	22188
233098	112197	251207	4206/7188
122953-A NGS	112338	276084	1978
122509-A NGS	112249	410769	11153